If you're like most young people, you like to be treated like an adult. Unfortunately, our society doesn't often tell us that with maturity comes responsibility for your own actions. By pointing out the costs and rewards of commitment to Christ, Fred Hartley shows you how to be a mature, dedicated Christian. In *100%*, he deals with the basics of discipleship—prayer... daily Bible reading ... trials and temptations ... witnessing ... obedience ... and spiritual warfare. Enthusiasm for Christ is *normal,* and 100% commitment is possible. *100%* gives you all the support, advice, and biblical instruction you need for becoming a joyful, productive disciple of Christ.

100%
Beyond Mediocrity

Fred Hartley

Illustrations by
Al Hartley

Fleming H. Revell Company
Old Tappan, New Jersey

Library of Congress Cataloging in Publication Data

Hartley, Fred.
   100%: beyond mediocrity.

   Summary: An invitation to the reader to make a "100%" commitment to Christianity. Uses anecdotes, sermons, and Bible excerpts.
   1. Youth—Religious life. [1. Christian life]
I. Title.   II. Title: One hundred percent.
BV4531.2.H348   1983   248.8′3   83-3349
ISBN 0-8007-5112-4

Contents

TO my elders

1
Go for It

Do you not know that in a race all the
runners compete, but only one receives
the prize? So run that you may obtain it.
1 Corinthians 9:24

IN ORDER to be good at anything, it requires commitment. And excellence requires 100 percent commitment. Nothing illustrates this as well as athletics.

Alberto Salazar is a name known only by a few sports fans and fellow long-distance runners. His twenty-three-year-old body is certainly not finished running, but in the 1982 Boston Marathon, he had the race of a lifetime.

It is Monday, April 19. The sun is out, and it is a balmy sixty-five degrees in downtown Boston. Salazar is favored to win, having walked off with first place from five other races this year, setting the marathon world record in New York in October, 1981 (2:08:13). That's what you call "quite a track record." There is only one problem: Twenty-five-year-old Dick Beardsley is not about to roll over and play dead. In fact, the gun fires, and Dick sets the pace. Salazar admitted after the race, "I could have slacked off. The pace was fast, probably too fast . . . The last seven miles or so, I was really feeling it [pain]."

Averaging almost thirteen miles an hour, Salazar and Beardsley stride along side by side, exchanging water bottles to keep their tongues from getting stuck to the roofs of their mouths. They strain to suck air. The marathon is called the most grueling of all athletic events because, in addition to having to dodge buses, motorcycles, and pedestrians, not to mention all the muscle cramps, dehydration, and fatigue, the runners surrender their bodies to such intense abuse for more than two hours.

Running side by side and leaving their guts along the 26 miles and 385 yards, Alberto Salazar crosses the finish line only two seconds before Beardsley. What a race! His face is milk white and stretched in agony as he collapses into the arms of two policemen. He needs water desperately, but he cannot drink. ("When he took water," his father told reporters, "he got cramps. When he didn't take any, he got dehydrated.")

You really have no idea what a long-distance runner goes through until you watch one cross the finish line and then keep watching for the next several minutes. In Boston in 1982, Dr. William Castelli headed the ninety-one-person medical team. Around him were stretchers, tubing, needles, intravenous bottles, wheelchairs, and cots. The doctor explained that besides the natural muscle strain, "For every fifteen minutes you're running, you need about eight ounces of fluid." It is no wonder that as the runners cross the finish line, they collapse with rock-hard muscle cramps or wrench in half with dry heaves. Those walking by frequently ask, "Why in the world do they do this to themselves?"

When Salazar finished a race in 1979, his temperature rose to 108 degrees, and he actually received last rites. Today, as he finishes in Boston, a nurse puts her hand under his arm, and he feels unusually cold. She takes his temperature, and it reads eighty-eight—hypothermia! He is taken to the medical room, and two intravenous feedings later, he begins to shake, and gradually his temperature rises.

Reflecting on a minimal two-second-margin victory, he says to the *Miami Herald*, "I really had to gut it out. Dick Beardsley is one of the toughest men I have ever run against. This was probably the hardest effort I have ever had to put into a race."

His dad, Jose Salazar, genuinely shaken over his son's condition, admits to the newspapermen, "One of these days he's going to kill himself. No question about it, he's going to destroy his life." He continues, "He told me never in his life had he made an effort like today. He suffered more than ever before, but he never thought of quitting. . . . This is the price you pay."

Yes, there is a price for winning: It is called *commitment*. It is often the single factor that separates the Varsity from the Junior Varsity, the A from the B+, and the gold medals from the *nice tries*. It is commitment that locks us in place, throws away the key, and says, "I don't care what it costs me, because I've already given it all I've got."

What about you? Are you committed to anything?

But I Don't Want to Lose

Anyone can run a race, but we take a risk when we try to win.

I was no Alberto Salazar, but in junior high there was a field day every spring from which I usually took home a few ribbons. One year the first competition was the 100-yard dash, which by some strange turn of events, I won. A blue ribbon! The second event was the mile run. I had never run the mile in my life. We all lined up on one side of the field and were told to run around the edge twice. Having just won the 100-yard dash, I lined up with delusions of grandeur—winning every event of the day!

Bang! The gun started the race, and I took off as if I were running another 100-yard dash. I couldn't understand why I was so far out in front of everyone else. As I neared the halfway point on the first lap I can remember feeling strong. A surge of adrenaline shot through my body as I ran past the bleachers and looked to see my girl friend cheering me on. (There is nothing like hearing your girl friend's voice as she screams your name at the top of her lungs!) I ran even faster. By the time I reached the end of the first lap, the next closest guy was at least 200 yards behind me. I was mentally licking my chops over the second blue ribbon.

In the next hundred yards, something happened. My legs started feeling like balloons filled with Jell-O. They wouldn't go where they were supposed to. My first response was to take the upper hand: "Come on, legs, just one more lap to go! You're way ahead—you can make it." I could hardly feel my legs. I tried with everything I had to run, but all I could do was swing my arms frantically and walk. At the time I didn't know it, but my body was trying to explain to me what happens when you run a mile at 100-yard-dash speed. I can still remember the first kid who passed me. And then the second, and third, and everyone else. That was humiliation at its worst. I was unable even to finish the race. When it was all over, there were more kids who came up to me, laughing at my exhaustion, than there were people giving congratulations to the winner.

That day I learned a powerful lesson about commitment. When you stand out in front of the pack, you are saying to the crowd, "I'm not just here to *run*, I'm here to *win*. Just watch. I'm going to give it all I've got, and I'll win." And when all I've got is not all I need, there is a real possibility for deep embarrassment. To run a race takes no guts, but to try to win is risky. All eyes were on me, and when I fell apart, everyone knew it.

Three years later, when I got together with some of my old friends, one of them recalled, "Hey, Fred, you remember when you blew a gasket trying to run that mile?" They all laughed. No one remembered the ribbons I had won, only the one I tried to win and lost.

The laughs really did not bother me. But I wonder about all the other kids who heard the laughs and said to themselves, *Man, I'm glad I'm not him. You'll never catch me out in front of the pack. That's dangerous!* I wonder about all the kids who don't try out for the team, fake sick on the day of the test, or stay home from the parties weekend after weekend, protecting themselves, like turtles, by withdrawing into their shells. It's safe, that's for sure. But it's also a drag.

I have a card on my desk. It shows a caricature of a turtle timidly sticking his awkward head from under his protective shell; under it the statement reads, "No guts, no glory."

I don't want to be a turtle, do you? Turtles don't often get hurt, but they don't do much either. Automobiles are their greatest enemies, and turtles often get smashed into the asphalt because they think they are protected as long as their heads are in their shells. Our fears often make us mediocre turtles. But we were never intended to live life in a shell.

Life requires that we take risks. If we are going to accomplish anything significant, there will always be the possibility of failure. No one likes to lose, but winning means that is a possibility.

Blah Is Not Beautiful

No one intentionally sets out to be ordinary. I have yet to meet anyone who likes to be called wallflower, run-of-the-mill, or plain Jane. You just don't sit down and say, "Now, let's see, what can I do to blend in and go unnoticed." But all it takes is a few cutting, cynical remarks against us, and we crawl back into our shells and hide. It can happen to the best of us, without our even realizing. We wake up one morning, and suddenly we realize that we are *blah.* We aren't good at anything.

"I failed at trombone lessons."
"I got cut from basketball because I couldn't make a lay-up."
"I am a straight C student (with an occasional B+ by the slime on my teeth)."
"I can get dates, but nobody will go out with me a second time."
"All my friends seem to have better friends."
"Even my dog would rather play with my sister."

Mediocre is when you're not bad; you're just not very good. It's commonplace, ordinary, average. It's the basic Rodney Dangerfield syndrome, and it's *gross!*

There is an alternative. There is a way to break out of our mediocrity and *go for it!*

The Price

Most of today's 25 million teenagers are not stupid. We know that anything that is worth much is going to cost us. A nice pair of Nike sneakers or Calvin Klein jeans are going to cost more than Brand X. The same is true in life; the achievements that we value have a price to them.

A car is a nice luxury, but there are the obligations of payments, gas, washing, and tune-ups.

Getting a driver's license is exciting. Getting a traffic ticket is a bummer. The *privileges* of having the license are balanced by the *responsibility* of using the freedom of driving within the restrictions of the law.

Breaking out of mediocrity is possible, if you are willing to pay the price of commitment. A commitment means, "I will enjoy these privileges as long as I meet my responsibilities." You can picture it as a scale with privilege on the one side, balanced by responsibilities on the other. (*See* illustration on page 13.)

Maturity is not always fun. It means, "I will assume full responsibility for my actions." It means, "I not only desire the privileges of adulthood, but I am willing to pay the price."

Let's Get Personal

Some comedian said, "There are three types of people in the world: Those who make things happen, those who watch things happen, and those who walk around trying to figure out what's happening." Don't laugh. It's true!

This book is designed to increase the number of people who make things happen.

When I was in high school, I met Jesus. One night, alone in my own room, I got down on my knees and prayed a very simple prayer. I said: "Jesus, I believe that when You died on the cross, You died for my sins. And I believe that You also rose from the dead and that You are alive

PRIVILEGE   RESPONSIBILITY

COMMITMENT

right now. I open my heart and ask You to come in and make me a new person. Thank You, Jesus."

Today I am convinced that Christianity without commitment is a sure loser. The greatest decision one will ever make is: What should I do with Jesus? I have come to the conclusion there are only two options: reject Him completely or follow Him 100 percent. Christianity is either worth everything, or it isn't worth a gum wrapper.

I meet thousands of teenagers every year, and many of them are close personal friends. I have yet to meet one who enjoys being treated like a baby. Well, this book will treat you like an adult, the way God treats you. There's just one thing; you cannot treat Jesus like a baby-sitter.

Since I did not like to read as a teen, I presume most teens do not like to read either. I have done everything I could to make this book easy to read. (In fact if it were any easier to read, it would talk to you.) Even though it is easy to read, it will not be easy to swallow.

Think

1. "Blah is not beautiful." In what ways have you settled for mediocrity in order to avoid the risk of being laughed at?
2. In your own words define *maturity*.
3. Have you noticed that there is a higher price tag for the things of greater value in life? (Give personal life examples.)
4. What commitments have you made? Do you find them difficult to keep?

Act

1. On a piece of paper list the most important things in your life, in order of importance. (Consider on what areas of your life you spend the most spare time? most money? most thought?)

   According to this list, to what are you committed? anything?
2. Ask a close friend or parent to tell you what he or she sees as the most important area of your life.

2
The Man

... What manner of man is this, that even
the wind and the sea obey him?
Mark 4:41 KJV

Jesus Christ is not a superstar. He's not like Burt Reynolds. He's not like Mohammed Ali, Elton John, or Reggie Jackson. Neither is He a fad. He's not a Rubik's Cube. He's not a skateboard. He's not a hula hoop or the latest video game.

The problem is, a few years ago, He became popular. According to George Gallup and his pollsters, 75 percent of all teenagers believe that Jesus is the Son of God and that He rose from the dead. Gallup concluded his report by saying, "American youth are all spiritually charged up, but they have no place to go."

"No place to go" all too clearly describes the average youth group: fun and games and prizes and recreation, but little life-changing substance. Too many kids are coming to the conclusion, "If this is what it means to follow Jesus, forget it!" Unfortunately I know more kids who have stopped following Jesus out of boredom than burnout. Unless we learn how to take the truths from between the leather covers of our Bibles and place them into the shoe leather of our daily lives, we might see the most intense antichrist movement in history from those who drop out. The reason Jesus is not a superstar is because superstars can become shooting stars.

Peeling Off the Skin

The real problem is this: People are rejecting Jesus before they really get to know Him. Mark Twain said, "The difference between what you believe and what you almost believe is the difference between lightning and the lightning bug." When someone looks at Jesus and says, "If that's God, who needs Him?" they are only rejecting the lightning bug.

My great-uncle who immigrated into our country more than a half century ago had never before seen a banana. He was told how good they were, so he bought a bunch, tore one off, and bit right into it. He chewed and chewed and chewed. Finally, due to the coarseness and bitterness, he spit it out. No one told him to peel off the skin first. Similarly, people are

16

turning off to Christ because of the skin, which often misrepresents the way Jesus really is.

Ronnie's dad was a preacher, and his mom taught his Sunday-school class. This meant every Sunday he got caught in crossfire.

One day I took him to the zoo, and he started to open up to me: "How would you feel if all you heard was, 'You can't do this,' and, 'You can't do that'? My parents think I'm a Christian. It would kill them to tell them any differently, but church is a boring drag. And heaven . . . who needs it? What am I going to do up there with a harp? No motorcycles! The whole thing just makes me sick."

Once he started, there was no stopping him.

"And the worst thing is my conscience. Wouldn't you know it, of all families to get stuck in, I'd have to be born into such a bunch of religious fanatics! Just look at it this way: I can't have any fun because they tell me it's sinful. When I go ahead and have some fun, I feel miserable anyway. So every weekend it's the same thing—stay home, watch TV, and get bored. Life is gross."

It was obvious to me that Ron was not rejecting Jesus. He was rejecting the banana peel. We need to get down to the real Jesus—the eternal Son of God, the One who blew people's minds when He was here on this planet, the One who still knows how.

The disciples hung around with Jesus, and they watched Him do amazing things. He:

Called evil spirits out of weird people.
Forgave sins.
Spoke to diseases, and the people were instantly healed.
Loved all people the same, regardless of race, religion, or social
bracket.

They saw Jesus do all these wonderful things for other people, but while traveling by boat in the middle of a bad storm, they got scared stiff. Their ship started to fill with water. Even though some were sailors, they thought they were going to sink and be lost at sea. Jesus, who had been sleeping, looked defiantly at the storm clouds and flatly said, "Peace! Be still!" Immediately the wind stopped blowing, and the sea got as smooth as a parking lot. As the bewildered disciples looked into one another's green faces they asked, "Who is this guy, that even the wind and the sea obey Him?" They had known Him. They had lived with Him, but suddenly the same Jesus who had done miracles for other people now worked a miracle for them that saved their lives, and they realized they needed to take a closer look.

Now is a good time for *us* to take a closer look at Jesus. After all, how can we give Him 100 percent if we don't even know who He is?

He Took Charge

Jesus exercised an awesome amount of authority. In the first chapter of Mark's gospel, we see Him begin His ministry with a bang. He took charge over all life:

Over *individual lives* by calling the disciples and expecting them to drop everything and follow Him (verses 16–20).
Over the *religious system* by teaching from the Scriptures in the synagogue with such boldness that the regular preachers were dumbfounded (verses 21, 22).
Over *demons* (verses 23–28).
Over sickness and the *human body* (verses 29–31).

In that single chapter we see nothing but nonstop authority. He acted as if He owned this place. (That's because He does.)

He Made Demands

I have been reading the Bible for sixteen years, but some things Jesus told people to do still make me wince. When He spoke, He expected people to listen. (Put a check next to the following statements that sound a little strong to you.)

"Follow me and I will make you become fishers of men."

Mark 1:17

". . . Go, sell what you have, and give to the poor. . . . It is easier for a camel to go through the eye of a needle than for a rich man to enter the kingdom of God."

Mark 10:21, 25

"... If any one would be first, he must be last of all and servant of all."

Mark 9:35

"And if your hand causes you to sin, cut it off; it is better for you to enter life maimed than with two hands to go to hell, to the unquenchable fire."

Mark 9:43

"No one who puts his hand to the plow and looks back is fit for the kingdom of God."

Luke 9:62

"... Lord, how often shall my brother sin against me, and I forgive him? As many as seven times?" Jesus said to him, "I do not say to you seven times, but seventy times seven."

Matthew 18:21, 22

"You, therefore, must be perfect, as your heavenly Father is perfect."

Matthew 5:48

"... Do not resist one who is evil. But if any one strikes you on the right cheek, turn to him the other also; and if any one would sue you and take your coat, let him have your cloak as well; and if any one forces you to go one mile, go with him two miles. Give to him who begs from you, and do not refuse him who would borrow from you."

Matthew 5:39–42

"If any one comes to me and does not hate his own father and mother and wife and children and brothers and sisters, yes, even his own life, he cannot be my disciple. . . . So therefore, whoever of you does not renounce all that he has cannot be my disciple."

Luke 14:26, 33

"If any man would come after me, let him deny himself and take up his cross and follow me."

Matthew 16:24

Obviously Jesus didn't play games with people. He drew straight lines and forced people to stand on one side or another, insisting, "He who is not with me is against me . . ." (Matthew 12:30).

What Jesus Thought of Himself

The reason Jesus made such demands on people is because of the way He saw Himself. Either Jesus was God, or He was the most stuck-up, conceited individual ever to set foot on the earth. Just listen to a few things He said:

"You search the scriptures, because you think that in them you have eternal life; and it is they that bear witness to *me.*"

John 5:39, *italics mine*

"*I* am the bread of life; he who come to *me* shall not hunger, and he who believes in *me* shall never thirst."

John 6:35, *italics mine*

"Truly, truly, *I* say to you, *I* am the door of the sheep."

John 10:7, *italics mine*

". . . *I* came that they may have life, and have it abundantly."

John 10:10, *italics mine*

"*I* am the good shepherd. . . ."

John 10:11, *italics mine*

"*I* am the resurrection and the life; he who believes in *me,* though he die, yet shall he live, and whoever lives and believes in *me* shall never die. . . ."

John 11:25, 26, *italics mine*

"And *I,* when *I* am lifted up from the earth, will draw all men to *myself.*"

John 12:32, *italics mine*

"I am the way, and the truth, and the life; no one comes to the Father, but by *me."*

John 14:6, *italics mine*

"I am [the Christ]; and you will see the Son of man seated at the right hand of Power, and coming with the clouds of heaven."

Mark 14:62, *italics mine*

Nobody fell asleep or even yawned when Jesus spoke, because they had never heard words like these from the lips of any man. It is not surprising that the religious leaders of His day did more than just scratch their heads when Jesus spoke about Himself. They tore their tunics, spit, screamed, and picked up rocks. They knew there were only two options: either He was who He said He was—the Almighty Son of God—or He was a puffed-up braggart who deserved the gas chamber for such blasphemy. There is no doubt about it: Jesus knew who He was, and He didn't mind telling anyone.

His Promises

Besides the wild claims He made about Himself and the outlandish things He did and the severe demands He made on all potential followers, Jesus offered some incredible benefits. If none of these impress you, you either don't understand what He is saying, or else you don't believe Him.

"Truly, truly, I say to you, he who believes in me will also do the works that I do; and greater works than these will he do, because I go to the Father."

John 14:12

"I will give you the keys of the kingdom of heaven, and whatever you bind on earth shall be bound in heaven, and whatever you loose on earth shall be loosed in heaven."

Matthew 16:19

"You are the salt of the earth. . . ."

Matthew 5:13

"You are the light of the world. . . ."

Matthew 5:14

"Blessed are you when men revile you and persecute you and utter all kinds of evil against you falsely on my account. Rejoice and be glad, for your reward is great in heaven. . . ."

Matthew 5:11, 12

". . . With God all things are possible."

Matthew 19:26

"You did not choose me, but I chose you and appointed you that you should go and bear fruit and that your fruit should abide; so that whatever you ask the Father in my name, he may give it to you."

John 15:16

"Hitherto you have asked nothing in my name; ask, and you will receive, that your joy may be full."

John 16:24

". . . I go and prepare a place for you, . . . that where I am you may be also."

John 14:3

"My sheep hear my voice, and I know them, and they follow me; and I give them eternal life, and they shall never perish, and no one shall snatch them out of my hand."

John 10:27, 28

"No longer do I call you servants, for the servant does not know what his master is doing; but I have called you friends. . . ."

John 15:15

Some of these promises are conditional and some are unconditional, but they are all promises.

Jesus not only expects a lot from His followers, but He richly rewards them:

"Truly, I say to you, there is no one who has left house or brothers or sisters or mother or father or children or lands, for my sake and for the gospel, who will not receive a hundredfold now in this time, houses and brothers and sisters and mothers and children and lands, with persecutions, and in the age to come eternal life."

Mark 10:29, 30

Will the Real Jesus Please Stand Up?

There is obviously only one Jesus. He is called the "only begotten Son" (John 3:16 KJV) and He is "the same yesterday and today and for ever" (Hebrews 13:8). Therefore, He is capable of taking charge of life, exercising authority, making demands, and giving benefits just as much today as during the days of His earth walk.

Our tendency is to see Him as older, more feeble, or less relevant—removed from real life. Such a shallow view of Jesus has disastrous effects on those who think they are following Him. Jesus is the Master Discipler, and if we are following Him, it is crucial to our welfare that we know Him accurately. If we have a shallow view of the Savior, we will have a shallow salvation. If we have a dwarf view of our Lord, we will have a dwarf commitment.

Last year I taught on the titles of Christ (of which there are more than 250). Besides the ones listed in the Bible, there is even reference to one that no one knows but Jesus Himself (Revelation 19:12). Jesus is far greater than our mortal minds will ever comprehend; yet because He spent part (thirty-three years) of His life on this planet, we have tangible evidence as to what He is like. He breathed and ate and cried and taught and sang and sweat and fished and hammered and sailed and slept just like a man. That is because He was a man. In fact, on the last day of His life, Pilate pointed at Jesus in front of the crowd and said, ". . . Behold the man!" (John 19:5). I wish on this day I could stand before you and, pointing to Jesus, say, "Behold the man!"

Not Religion, but a Relationship

Jesus made it clear that He was not here just to tell men to be good. Neither was He here to start a new religion. The key to His teaching was that He came to build a relationship with people. This is obvious by the things He did for people and the things He said to people.

Things He Did

Jesus told the woman caught in adultery, "Neither do I condemn you; go, and do not sin again" (John 8:11).

He frequently took children in His arms to bless them, even though His disciples thought it was a foolish waste of time (Mark 10:13–16).

When His close friend Mary anointed His feet with perfume, again He had to calm His uptight disciples, who thought the kind gesture was too extravagant (John 12:1–8).

Contrary to all social standards, one day Jesus talked with a woman (strike one), Samaritan (strike two), who was out fetching her own water (strike three), because He was so concerned for her soul (John 4:7–39).

He hung around with so many town bums and social misfits that He got the nicknames *glutton* and *drunkard*.

Jesus was more concerned about loving and accepting people, regardless of background and social standing, than He was in starting some formal, stuffy religion. By His life He showed that He was reaching out to people, not just to help them, but to build personal relationships with them.

Things He Said

"For the Son of man came not to be served but to serve, and to give his life as a ransom for many."

Mark 10:45

"Come to me, all who labor and are heavy laden, and I will give you rest. Take my yoke upon you, and learn from me; for I am gentle and lowly in heart, and you will find rest for your souls. For my yoke is easy, and my burden is light."

Matthew 11:28–30

"Behold, I stand at the door and knock; if any one hears my voice and opens the door, I will come in to him and eat with him, and he with me."

Revelation 3:20

". . . I will never fail you nor forsake you."

Hebrews 13:5

If you add all this up, you will understand that Jesus wants to have personal relationships with His people—so personal that He wants to call us "friends."

First Things First

It makes no sense to start talking about surrendering your life to Jesus until you know you can trust Him with it. After all, it is the only one you've got. This is why He said, "And this is life eternal, that they might *know* thee the only true God, and Jesus Christ whom thou hast sent" (John 17:3 KJV, *italics mine*). Knowing Jesus and having eternal life go hand in hand. You don't have one without the other.

Have you met Him? Are you more a follower of Him today than when you first met Him? Or have you crumpled Him up like a letter from your old girl friend and thrown Him in the trash because something bigger and better has come into your life? Even worse, have you let Him just sit in the closet and collect dust?

Jesus never called anyone just to sit around and look pretty. And He certainly never called anyone just to sit around and look bored. Being a Christian doesn't mean that you have to wear a powder blue leisure suit, shave your beard, and talk in cliches. That's because Christianity isn't a lot of words. Neither is it an outward show. Christianity is Jesus! It is a relationship with a man who died for us two thousand years ago and who lives for us today.

Check this out: *It doesn't cost you anything to* become *a Christian, but it sure costs you something to* be *a Christian. In fact it costs everything.* If you have been a follower of Jesus and have never heard that before, you've been lied to. There *is* a cost to discipleship.

Perhaps you asked Jesus into your heart when you were a child or as a teen—perhaps only recently. Regardless, here are a few questions for you:

Is your life-style morally different from your friends' at school?
Have you overcome your bad habits, or are you at least trying?
When you read the Bible, can you understand what you read?
Do you have a daily time of prayer? Are you seeing specific answers?
Can you tell your friends about Jesus without feeling embarrassed?

If you cannot answer a strong yes to each of the above questions, consider yourself average and be glad there is plenty of room for improvement.

To a generation that watches an average of forty hours of TV a week and puts 32 billion quarters in video games every year, a book that tells you that following Jesus is not always a bowlful of cherries might sound too much like work. There's just one thing: One day soon Jesus is coming with all His angelic Space Invaders to unplug all the TV sets and video games. Then we will find out who are really His and who were just playing games.

Isn't it about time we stopped goofing around with Jesus and started taking Him seriously? Deep down we know that if Jesus is worth anything, He's worth everything.

Jesus is not a Rubik's Cube, nor is He a superstar. He's the Almighty Son of God. He is Lord of lords and King of kings. But the question is: Who is He to *you?*

The number-one mark of a Christian is knowing Jesus. Do you know Him? He knows you.

Think

1. Having read this chapter, how has your view of Jesus changed?
2. What does Jesus want from you? What does it mean to follow Him?
3. What are some false definitions of a *Christian?* What is an accurate definition?
4. What does it cost to *become* a Christian? What does it cost to *be* a Christian?

Act

1. If you have never talked to Jesus, it's about time! Be honest with Him.

If you believe He is whom He said He is (the Son of God), tell Him.

Admit to Him that you have messed up—sinned.

Thank Him for dying on the cross for you, personally.

Since He has been raised from the dead and is alive right now, you can ask Him to come into your life.

Place your life (100 percent) in His hands and ask Him to take charge.

2. Memorize Matthew 16:24 (word perfect). Quote it every day this week, thinking about what it really means to follow Jesus.

Read

If you still want to look more at the man Jesus, read the gospel of John, asking the question, "Who is He?" (Be sure to read John 20:31.) You should be able to make a list of at least one dozen different titles for Jesus.

3
Total (Not Toadal) Commitment

... Choose this day whom you will
serve....
Joshua 24:15

Toads are sort of like frogs, except they are fatter, slower, uglier, shier, and toothless. Toads hide from the light, waiting until the sun goes down before they come out. They live in damp places where they hunt slugs, insects, and worms. They have short, fat legs that can barely move. When winter comes, they dig a hole in the mud and hibernate. There are over seventy different species of toads. Living in south Florida, I see them everywhere. Being a jogger, I see most of them flattened and dried like pancakes on the pavement.

Toadal commitment has spread like warts among the Christian community. It can be distinguished from *total commitment* by being fatter, slower, uglier, shier, and toothless. Those who fall in this category tend to hide from the light, not wanting to get overexposed to the truth of God's Word. They prefer living in the dark, damp places and eating weird things. They have short legs that keep them from getting off the ground, and they frequently go into hibernation for long periods of time, during which they show little or no signs of real life. Those who have made a toadal commitment can be divided into many different species, but they are all harmless. They have no teeth and no major defense mechanism other than their blahness. They are so ugly, most people just keep their distance. Once in a while they will get caught underfoot and smashed into the pavement, but there is no great loss.

On the other hand, total commitment is disciplined, well trained, attractive, outgoing, aggressive, and potentially dangerous. Those who fall into this category love the light, and as children of the light, they have left their deeds of darkness and feed only on the pure Word of God. They are trained and fit for every good work, with the strength of Almighty God pumping through their well-toned muscles. They are quick and active, readily responsive to the voice of their Master. But because they have a master, those without one will call them fanatics and will consider them dangerous and offensive. There will be those who will try to stamp out the totally committed, but they won't be able to, because nobody steps on God's fingers, and that's where He keeps them.

The two words sound alike, but there are miles separating toadal and total commitment.

Mediocrity is the curse to commitment. It sinks its fangs into the neck and sucks the lifeblood right out of would-be world changers.

Its foul voice whispers things like:

"You don't want to take things too seriously, everything in moderation."

"God isn't concerned with those common sins; nobody's perfect."

"You don't want to stick out."

"Wait until you're older before you decide to follow Jesus."

So we have mediocre holiness, mediocre prayer, mediocre obedience, mediocre love, mediocre Bible reading, mediocre worship, and mediocre Christianity. But mediocrity stinks like a fried toad.

Broken Commitment

Our society is great at breaking commitments.

Every year 2 million couples stand before a minister or justice of the peace and commit themselves to each other "For richer for poorer, in sickness and in health, to have and to hold, from this time forth . . ." and all that good stuff. And every year almost 2 million couples break that commitment in divorce or separation.

Every year I speak at youth camps, and sometimes it is discouraging to see the same kids, year after year, who made very serious commitments previous years, but who never even came close to living up to their commitments.

I read a statistic the other day: 90 percent of the kids who commit themselves to Christ to pursue a career in missionary service never get to the mission field.

Mark Twain hit the nail on the thumb when he said, "It's easy to stop smoking; I've done it a thousand times."

There is nothing wrong with making commitments to Christ. I try to commit myself to Him every day. The problem comes when we break the ones we've made.

Counting the Cost

When I was in high school, I begged my parents to buy me a myna bird. They would not budge. I read all kinds of bird books, raised enough money to buy it myself, and even promised to take care of it and feed it daily. Finally after months of persuasion, they said, "Okay."

When I brought that bird home, it was great. I talked to it constantly. "Hello, my name is Mildred, Mildred the myna bird. Hello, say hello. . . ." She wouldn't say anything, just squawked in my face.

I had read how messy they were, but it blew my mind when she soaked through three layers of newspaper in the bottom of the cage. You see, all they eat is fruit. The more fruit they eat, the messier they are. Besides the mess in the bottom of the cage, the floor and wall near the cage were a veritable fruit salad. Even though I had begged and begged for a myna bird, I did not know what I was getting myself into.

One weekend when I returned with some friends from a camping trip, I went up to my room and flopped on my bed, exhausted. When I awoke, my mother asked me if I noticed anything different. I told her I didn't, and she went out of the room, giggling. Then my father came in with a big smile and asked, "Do you notice anything different?" When I told him I didn't, he handed me forty dollars and laughed, "We sold the bird!"

At first I was embarrassed, then mad, then relieved. That dumb little bird turned out to be too big to handle. I will never be able to look at another myna bird without looking at the bottom of the cage. Having the bird was fun, but caring for it was a burden.

Jesus told His followers to count the cost before they made a commitment. One day He turned to the crowd—a huge crowd—and laid it right on the line:

"If any one comes to me and does not hate his own father and mother and wife and children and brothers and sisters, yes, and even his own life, he cannot be my disciple. Whoever does not bear his own cross and come after me, cannot be my disciple. For which of you, desiring to build a tower, does not first sit down and count the cost, whether he has enough to complete it? Otherwise, when he has laid a foundation, and is not able to finish, all who see it begin to mock him, saying, 'This man began to build, and was not able to finish.' Or what king going to encounter another king in war, will not sit down first and take counsel whether he is able with ten thousand to meet him who comes against him with twenty thousand? And if not, while the other is yet a great way off, he sends an embassy and asks terms of peace. So therefore, whoever of you does not renounce all that he has cannot be my disciple."

Luke 14:26–33

Jesus does not want any of us to be dropouts. He wants us to think through our commitment and to recognize that since there are such great benefits, there are obviously some responsibilities. (Remember the scale?)

A Covenant Written in Blood

At the heart of our relationship with God is commitment. The Bible uses the word *covenant.* When we take communion, we often hear the words of Jesus as He served the wine at His last meal, "This cup is the new covenant in my blood."

Ordinarily, a covenant is considered an agreement or commitment entered into by two people. In the New Testament there are two different words used for "covenant." The Greek word *syntheke* is used to describe the marital covenant between two equals, while *diatheke* is used to describe God's covenant with man, literally meaning not so much a "covenant" but a "will." A will is made by one person to be accepted by another person, who cannot alter the terms and who could never have made the will in the first place.

At the heart of our relationship with God is a word that sums it all up—"covenant," *diatheke.* We do not meet on equal terms. Obviously we couldn't—He's God! It was up to Him to make the first move, which He did in Jesus. He offers us an intimate relationship that we cannot alter, change, or annul, but which we can only accept or reject.

When He established this new covenant, it involved a 100 percent commitment.

He was born 100 percent human.
He lived 100 percent dedicated to God.
He died 100 percent.

Therefore "the new covenant in my blood" is a 100 percent commitment of God to us. This is why it doesn't cost us a nickel to become a Christian. In fact, we won't get anywhere with God until we realize we can't earn His favor. But once we are Christians, it costs us everything.

Jesus doesn't say, "If you commit yourself to Me, I will commit Myself to you." He says, "I have already committed Myself to you 100 percent, period." And He looks at us as if to say, *Now, what are you going to do about it?*

Anyone who would reject such an offer as this deserves to be damned.

I look at the cross and see a man who gave 100 percent, and I look at His people and see such mediocrity and fall to my knees crying, "Where are the fanatics You died for? Where are the ones You raised from the dead? You who totally committed Yourself to us, where are the ones who are like You in their commitment?"

An Example

C. T. Studd grew up in England. He was a great athlete, a star cricket player who made headlines throughout his country. (Cricket is not something you do with grasshoppers; it's like baseball.) Academically he was at the top of his class. He was from a wealthy family and always had the best of everything. When he met Jesus, he said, "If Jesus be God and He died for me, there is no sacrifice too great for me to make for Him." (Read that again.)

Prior to his marriage, he gave away half his fortune, which at the time was equal to $20,000 in United States currency. (Today worth close to $200,000.) When his fiancée learned he only gave one-half of it away, she asked, "Charlie, what did the Lord tell the rich young man to do?" "Sell all," he answered. "Well, we, too, will start clear with the Lord at our wedding." All the money went overseas to missions.

It wasn't long before they moved to Africa to give their lives to Jesus in missionary service. C. T. Studd lived his life according to a principle we all need to apply, "If Jesus be God and He died for me, there is no sacrifice too great for me to make for Him."

What Is Normal?

We have accepted the idea, "What is mediocre is average, what is average is normal, what is normal is good. Therefore, what is mediocre is good." With such a warped viewpoint, when a person who is enthusiastic about Jesus comes along with a 98.6-degree temperature, we think he is sick.

When Lori met Jesus, she was on fire. She carried her Bible not only to church and youth meetings, but to school. She was one of the only kids who sang all the choruses and volunteered to pray out loud. She loved Jesus so much she told all her friends about Him and even embarrassed some of the other Christian kids. She visited some of the elderly people in the church and brought them cookies.

The other kids in the group started getting aggravated and told her things like:

"Don't worry, it will wear off after you've been a Christian for a while."
"Be careful, you don't want to come on too strong."
"Everything in moderation—you don't want to go overboard."

I heard all these same ideas when I was a young Christian, and I cringed. They all smacked of status-quo mediocrity.

Well, I have news for you: We are followers of the One who said, "For zeal for thy house has consumed me . . ." (Psalms 69:9) and who says of us "I will make my ministers flames of fire" (*see* Psalms 104:4).

Zeal is normal for a Christian.
It is normal to give 100 percent to the One who gave 100 percent for us.
It is impossible to be too Jesus centered.

When Lori came to me, concerned about what the others were telling her, I told her what godly counselors told me: "Keep your eyes on Jesus, not on people. People will always let you down, but Jesus says, 'I will never fail you nor forsake you.'"

Lori poured her energies into Christ, through her high-school years, and developed into a dynamic disciple. Today she is a more faithful follower of Christ than she was even during her teenage years.

Keeping Commitments

One of the hardest things to deal with in keeping commitments is dealing with past failures. We hate to fail.

This summer we tried to teach my five-year-old son to water ski. He is strong enough and fairly coordinated, but he has one problem—he doesn't like to fall! How do you expect a five-year-old to learn to water ski, if he's afraid to fall?

Some of us have the same problem with following Jesus. We would rather not recommit ourselves to Him, just so that we don't fail Him like last time. We say, "I don't want to be a hypocrite." But there is a difference between a failure and a faker. A *faker* is someone who acts as if he is a Christian, when he isn't. A *failure* is someone who acts as if he isn't a Christian, when he is.

The devil is "the accuser of the brethren," and he loves to accuse us of not being truly born-again children of God. So many have said to me, "I want to follow Jesus, but I feel like such a faker!" Usually, they aren't fakers; they are failures—genuine Christians who have problems living consistently. Jesus' friend Peter was a failure. He was certainly not a faker; no one was more earnest than Peter. Sure he blew it—three times! But Jesus loved him and gave him the grace to forgive himself.

Faithful is he that calleth you, who also will do it.

1 Thessalonians 5:24 KJV

... He who began a good work in you will bring it to completion....

Philippians 1:6

> If we are faithless, he remains faithful—for he cannot deny himself.
>
> 2 Timothy 2:13

The reason Jesus can keep His commitment and help us keep ours is because He has already committed Himself 100 percent. The quicker we understand that, the sooner we will be able to do the same for Him.

General William Booth, founder of the Salvation Army, said, "Reservations are the damnation of our consecration." Jesus gave Himself for you completely. Will you give yourself without reservation to Him?

When you pick a college, you say no to every other university and yes to just one. When you get married, you say no to the other 2.5 billion possible spouses and yes exclusively to one. God tells us we must make that same choice with Him: ". . . Choose this day whom you will serve" (Joshua 24:15).

Consecration is handing God a blank sheet with your name signed on the bottom, to fill in any way He wants. Right now might be a good time. "If Jesus be God and He died for me, there is no sacrifice too great for me to make for Him."

Think

1. Make your own list of characteristics for *toadal commitment*. For *total commitment*.
2. What keeps us from completely surrendering ourselves to Jesus?
3. "Broken commitments keep us from making new commitments." Have you found that true in relation to following Jesus?
4. What sort of commitment (covenant) has Jesus made with us?

Act

Memorize Romans 12:1, 2 (word perfect) and quote it through the week.

Read

For the whole story on C. T. Studd, I highly recommend this exciting biography: Norman Grubb, *C. T. Studd* (Fort Washington, Pa.: Christian Literature Crusade, 1972).

4
No Padded Crosses

"If any man would come after me, let
him deny himself and take up his cross
and follow me."
Matthew 16:24

The cross has been the symbol of Christians for centuries. It is brass in churches, diamond studded on necklaces, cut from stone in cemeteries. Unfortunately it is all too often foam-rubber padded in our daily lives. The symbol of Christianity is not a cushion, but the cross.

Jesus did not say, "Take up your queen-size mattress." He said, "If any man would come after me, let him deny himself and take up his cross and follow me" (Matthew 16:24).

Why the cross? There is only one three-letter answer to why Jesus had to hang on it: *sin.* I believe the single reason our country is raising such a crop of pygmy Christians is because we are afraid of that little, big word. It may look small—small enough to overlook—but that's what was said about the iceberg by the helmsman on the *Titanic.* If it was big enough to nail Jesus to the tree, it's big enough to deserve our attention.

Is Sin Fun?

For too long we have thought the cross was for the unsaved sinners. It's for the saved sinners, too.

I had been counseling with Paul for almost two months. He would frequently repent for things done while dating, and he would make resolutions about avoiding such pitfalls in the future. But the problem continued for too long, so I felt it was time to draw the line.

"You need to quit playing games with your emotions. You've been having problems for too long to do something stupid like being alone in her home at night."

"But we love each other," he interrupted. "How can it be wrong when it feels so right?" (He almost sounded like Debbie Boone.)

We talked some more, and Paul made some more resolutions, but it obviously didn't do much good. You see, even as I am writing these words not I or his parents or any of his friends know where he is. He ran away with his girl friend and left the state.

Paul, like hundreds of thousands of other sincere Christian young people, has this strange idea: "As long as Jesus lives inside me, anything I feel like doing must be A-okay with Him." Before we know it, we have adopted the "if it feels good, do it" philosophy.

Question: Is sin fun? (a) Yes (b) No (c) Some of the time

Answer: (c) ǝɯıʇ ǝɥʇ ɟo ǝɯoS

The devil spreads the lie that sin is *not* fun. After all, if sin is not fun, then anything that is fun is not sin. So if it feels good, do it!

Obviously not all sin is fun. It's wrong to harm yourself, and I don't know many who enjoy slamming their feet with sledge hammers.

But when are we going to get it through our thick heads that often sin is fun? The Bible talks about ". . . the fleeting pleasures of sin" (Hebrews 11:25). The problem starts when the fun thing we desire to do is the very same thing that is wrong and harmful. "For the desires of the flesh are against the Spirit, and the desires of the Spirit are against the flesh; for these are opposed to each other, to prevent you from doing what you would" (Galatians 5:17).

If we follow our feelings, before we know it, we can get sucked like lint into a vacuum. What *feels good* does not equal what *is good.* Good can feel bad, and bad can feel very good. There is a higher standard by which we need to judge right from wrong: the Bible. (The next chapter explains how to read the Bible and not only understand it, but live it!)

Getting Nailed

With no apologies, the Bible tells us exactly what to do when we locate some activity in our lives that is out of line. Jesus expects us to take off our shirts, lie back down on the cross, stretch out our arms, and get nailed. Willful crucifixion is a mark of a Christian.

Jesus told His followers that each must ". . . take up his cross daily . . ." (Luke 9:23).

Paul was so accustomed to getting nailed to the tree, he wrote, "I have been crucified with Christ; it is no longer I who live, but Christ who lives in me; and the life I now live in the flesh, I live by faith in the Son of God, who loved me and gave himself for me" (Galatians 2:20).

Right now my wife is discipling a girl who has become an expert at choosing the cross. I could fill an encyclopedia with example after example of different situations in which she obeyed what God wanted her to do, even when everything inside her said, "Don't do it." This girl has become thoroughly obedient to her parents and has led them to Christ. She has frequently confessed sin and asked forgiveness from friends she had offended, reads the Bible daily, and shares her faith at school despite much opposition. Before each step of obedience, she fought and resisted, because the cross is never comfortable. But when she recognizes it as another case of her will against Jesus', she submits and, where necessary, repents. Although the cross is no more comfortable for her than for anyone else, she doesn't mind choosing it. God has taught her that His way always *is* best, even when it doesn't *feel* best.

Billy Sunday was a preacher who was willing to do anything to hold his audience's attention: lie down, throw chairs, fire six-shooters. He didn't mind offending people, either. "They say I rub the fur the wrong way. I don't. I just tell that cat to turn around!"

The first word preached by John the Baptist was *repent.* The first word preached by Jesus was *repent.* The climax of the first Christian sermon preached by Peter at Pentecost was *repent.* They all told their audiences to turn around.

"Get Down Off That Cross!"

Jesus was the first man in all history to get crucified who could have gotten down if He wanted. Even the crowds screamed, "Get down off that cross!" But He hung there.

Now as all believers face the cross, we have worldly wisdom and our own evil desires echoing the same scream, "Get down off that cross!" There is just one problem: Without the cross, there is no Christianity. It's even possible to hang around the cross without getting nailed to it.

The other day a sixteen-year-old girl told me, "Man, when I became a Christian, all they told me was, 'Ask Jesus into your heart, and you will go to heaven.' *Why not?* I thought. *Who doesn't want to go to heaven?* So I did. But now I can't stand it. I feel guilty all the time. I like smoking grass and sleeping with my boyfriend. Nobody's going to tell me what to do." She didn't want anything to do with the cross, so she rejected the man who hung there.

Mickey Cohen was a well-known gangster. When he attended an evangelistic service, some sincere Christian men made contact with him, thinking it would be a great testimony if he would get saved. During their meeting, Cohen said a prayer indicating his desire to be a Christian and to go to heaven. The men left all excited, because this famous thief had prayed to accept Christ.

Later when they talked with him about changing his life-style, he emphatically rejected the idea. If there were Christian athletes and Christian businessmen and Christian authors, he reasoned, why not Christian gangsters?

Talk is cheap. I once heard a bird say he was George Washington. Anyone can say he is a Christian, but Jesus is very concerned that we live like one. And there is only one way to live the Christian life—to deliberately choose the cross. Jesus did it, and we are to do it, too.

The Murder

"I wish I didn't have to be the one to make this announcement. It is very serious, and I don't want anyone to leave the auditorium until this matter is settled. Other years there has been money stolen, firecrackers, some broken curfews. But this year I have it on very good authority: *There is a murderer here,*" I began my talk to 200 kids at summer camp.

All at once everyone took a big gulp of air, and then it seemed as if no one even breathed. Every eye stared at me, without a blink.

"I don't want anyone to leave; it's dark outside, and there is a killer among us here at the camp. It is essential that we deal with the killer."

After a long pause I added, "My authority is the Bible. It tells us who the murderer is—his name is *sin.*"

Naturally the kids were temporarily relieved that the murderer was not one of their fellow campers. However, before the evening was through, dozens of teens came for prayer and public repentance, because they learned that the murderer was even closer to them than a fellow camper: The murderer lived within them.

There is a way which seems right to a man, but its end is the way to death.

Proverbs 14:12

... The wages of sin is death. ...

Romans 6:23

... You were dead through the trespasses and sins.

Ephesians 2:1

In order for you to dramatically understand what the Bible is saying, imagine the following:

Every time you lie, you immediately start getting a gigantic tumor on your tongue.
Whenever you look at someone lustfully, you start going blind.
When you steal something, your hand immediately turns leprous.
When you get proud, you have a heart attack.
Each time you swear, one of your lungs collapses.

If there were such a visible relationship between physical death and spiritual disobedience, we'd all be in a lot of trouble, but it sure wouldn't take us long to repent.

Deadly Ungratefulness

The worst murder sin ever committed was when it killed Jesus. Yet we still treat the cross so glibly.

Several years ago a high-school class in Australia took a field trip along a river. All the students were asked to stick close together because of the steep riverbank and the driving current. There was one boy, Billy, the class clown, who deliberately ran, unnoticed, away from his classmates. Eventually someone recognized his absence. Just then, from the rushing waters, they heard screaming and splashing. Billy had lost his footing and had fallen into the river. The headmaster immediately jumped in, swam to the helpless boy, and using all his energy, wrestled him to shore. The bank was high, so he lifted Billy up to the outstretched arms of his classmates. No sooner was Billy safe on land than the headmaster was swept out into the rushing waters. As he gasped for air he sucked in water and drowned.

A few days later a friend came to visit Billy to see how he was doing after such a dramatic rescue. "You must be indebted to your headmaster for giving his own life for you?"

Billy responded, "Ah, that old goat! If he had any brains, he would have let me drown." The friend walked away, shocked at such ungratefulness.

Pathetically Jesus often gets treated like that headmaster. He jumped in to save us from our helpless condition. In lifting us up out of sin and death, He Himself was crucified. But, shockingly, so often we show no gratitude to Him for what He has done. That is not normal. In fact it is obscene!

Dead Center

The cross is right at the heart—dead center—of Christianity. Without it, you might be having a good time, but you don't have Jesus. It is normal for a Christian to love the cross: first, because our Lord and Savior died there, and second, because it is where we, too, learn obedience by ourselves dying to sin.

Paul put it this way, "But far be it from me to glory except in the cross of our Lord Jesus Christ, by which the world has been crucified to me, and I to the world" (Galatians 6:14). The cross not only got him excited; it was the only thing that got him excited. And there was no foam-rubber padding. It was hard, rough wood, but full of the love of Jesus.

Jesus gives us, as His followers, an opportunity to know the cross:

By obeying and honoring our parents, even when they seem too narrow-minded.

By saying no to our boyfriends or girl friends who threaten to leave unless we have sex.

By quitting grass, even though we still feel like smoking.

By telling our friends about Jesus, even when we think for sure they won't understand.

The cross will always be the symbol of vibrant Christianity; it's the heart of what Jesus did for us, and it's the place where He calls us every day.

What has He asked you to do lately that you didn't feel like doing?

Think

1. Define *sin*.
2. Which sin is most active in your life?
3. Why is sin sometimes fun?
4. What is the importance of the cross in the life of a Christian? Explain the phrase "willful crucifixion."

Act

1. From Exodus 20:1–17 make a list of the Ten Commandments. Since you have broken each of them (either mentally or physically), think about your personal sinfulness in light of each one.
2. In order to appreciate the death of Jesus on the cross, imagine being the one who drove nails through His hands and feet.
3. Any specific sins that are still active must be rooted out and put to death. It is important to deal with the most obnoxious sin first. Since your sins died with Christ on the cross, personalize the following Bible verse by inserting your name where appropriate:

I,———, have been crucified with Christ; it is no longer I,———, who live, but Christ who lives in me; and the life I,———, now live in the flesh, I,———, live by faith in the Son of God, who loved me and gave himself for me.

Galatians 2:20

4. Memorize Romans 3:10–18 (word perfect) and meditate on how depraved our hearts are apart from Christ.

Read

To see a man who has experienced the cross, read Charles Colson's *Born Again* (Old Tappan, N. J.: Fleming H. Revell, 1977) especially chapter eight, "An Unforgettable Night." To go back a thousand years, one of the most dynamic personal testimonies of all time, is Augustine's *Confessions* (NY: Penguin, 1961).

5
No Dusty Bibles

"... If you continue in my word, you are
truly my disciples."
John 8:31

If all the unused Bibles were picked up at one time, there would probably be a dust storm so severe that it would block out the sun.

There are many reasons Bible reading gets placed at the bottom of our list of things to do:

"I don't have enough time."
"I don't understand what I'm reading—get lost in all *thees* and *thous.*"
"It's boring."
"I have more important things to do."
"I just don't like to read."

Despite all the reasons against doing it, Jesus said there is no substitute. Either we read the Bible daily, or somehow we are cheating ourselves.

Quiet Time, Boring Time

The idea of spending fifteen minutes every day all alone in a room, with nothing but the Bible, causes some kids to hyperventilate. "No TV? No FM radio? No stereo headphones? You've got to be joking. If that's what you call *quiet time,* it sounds to me more like *boring* time!"

I doubt whether it would be boring for any of us to be in a room for fifteen minutes alone with Brooke Shields or Tracy Austin or Bruce Jenner or O. J. Simpson. I'm sure we would find plenty of things to talk about. We wouldn't need TV or stereo. Why, then, do we yawn at the possibility of spending fifteen minutes alone with God?

Could it be that we are not impressed with God, as if He has no great accomplishments?
Maybe we are not sure He even exists or that, if He does exist, He would certainly have better things to do than mess around with us.

Perhaps the reason is that our minds are so easily distracted, and since God is invisible, He's hard to talk to—He doesn't audibly talk back or answer when we ask Him a question.

If we were honest with ourselves, it might even be because we don't really want to hear what He has to say.

How Is Your Appetite?

A growing young person who is not hungry is either sick or in love. Usually even being in love can't curb a teenage appetite. I knew a kid who would empty a half-gallon of ice cream into a bowl, pour a whole can of Hershey's chocolate syrup over it, and eat it as a midnight snack. This same kid ate four large pizzas on a dare. Healthy young people have ferocious appetites.

Healthy Christians have ferocious appetites, too. You don't have to tell a healthy Christian to read the Bible. Just as a healthy teen will gladly wolf down food, so a healthy Christian will feed on the Word. He will be glad to sacrifice snacks, sleep, and social events in order to eat the Wonder Bread—the Word of God.

You don't eat one meal a week or a month. You eat every day. Growing, healthy teenagers eat almost constantly. That's the way Jesus says it should be for us in God's Word. He said it is the mark of every Christian to continue in His Word.

A vitamin is a substance needed by your body, which your body cannot produce for itself. That sounds just like the Bible. Vitamins do for the body what the Bible does for the soul. Unfortunately we cannot simply condense God's Word down into a capsule to be taken orally, like a One-A-Day. Neither can it be put into a serum to be drawn into a syringe and injected like a main line into our system. A quick fix doesn't make it. God has shown Himself to us in His Word, and He expects us to feed on it regularly. There are no shortcuts; it takes a deliberate, daily effort, even when the hunger cramps aren't there.

Danger: High Explosives

It makes me sick to hear anyone say, "The Bible is boring." It's not boring. It's the Word of God! We are eager to:

Read comics to find what Archie or Doonesbury says.
Listen to the news to hear what Dan Rather says.
Watch press conferences to hear what our president says.
Attend the concert to hear what the rock singer says.

But we don't care what Almighty God says!

Like TNT or nitroglycerin, the Bible is powerful stuff. "Is not my word like fire, says the Lord, and like a hammer which breaks the rock in pieces?" (Jeremiah 23:29). The problem is, often our hearts are like granite. Even a lightning bolt will bounce off a rock. The Word seems to bounce off without making any necessary change.

Voltaire thought the Bible was useless. He said, "If we would destroy the Christian religion, we must first of all destroy man's belief in the Bible." He further predicted that within 100 years Christianity would be gone. Ironically, within 50 years, Voltaire's house was owned by the Swiss Bible Society, and it was full of Bibles! God will always have the last laugh.

When Noel Paul Stookey of the folk group Peter, Paul, and Mary was going through a time of searching and crisis, being disturbed with hypocrisy in his life, he asked his Greenwich Village friend, Bob Dylan, for advice.

Two things that Dylan told Paul stood out in his mind: go for a long walk in the country and read the Bible. Paul took the advice. He walked in the country, and it helped him sort out his priorities. And he read the Bible. Although his famous folk group had sung spirituals and gospel tunes, Stookey had never before opened a Bible. He read through the entire New Testament and parts of the Old. As he read the Bible it was slow going and at times mysterious, but gradually he became convinced that there was such a thing as absolute truth. Having this groundwork done by God's Word, when he met real, live Christians who explained that Jesus loved him personally, he was ready to accept Christ. Today Noel Stookey is living for Jesus because the Word of God did its faithful demolition job on his hard, unbelieving heart.

If reading the Bible seems like a vain, useless chore, I have some good news and some bad news. The good news is, there is nothing wrong with the Bible. The bad news is, there is something wrong with you. You need to keep exposing that hard, unbelieving heart of yours to the highly explosive Word of God.

Wash Those Old Brains

Jesus prayed, "Sanctify them in the truth; thy word is truth" (John 17:17). *Sanctify* means "to make holy." Jesus wants His followers to be holy, and one of the primary scrub brushes given to His disciples is His Word.

Contemporary songwriter and musician Barry McGuire was accused by some of his friends of getting brainwashed by reading the Bible too much. He answered back by simply saying, "That's okay, my old brains were so dirty they needed to get washed."

Barry doesn't apologize for reading the Bible, because it was through reading the Bible that he met Jesus. He figured if he met Jesus through reading the Bible, it would help him live like Him, too.

When we meet Jesus and repent from our old way of life, Jesus wants us to start living differently. In order to live differently, we need to think differently—to look at life from an entirely new perspective. As the aggressive apostle Paul said, "Do not be conformed to this world but be transformed by the renewal of your mind . . ." (Romans 12:2). There is only one way to unscramble our brains—to think God's thoughts. After all, "For my thoughts are not your thoughts, neither are your ways my ways, says the Lord" (Isaiah 55:8). And there is only one way to think God's thoughts: to read and obey the Bible.

Scalpel, Please

The Bible is like a surgeon's knife that skillfully and gently slices diseased areas out of our lives. Not just any old tools will do.

I had heard rumors that one of my Christian friends had been getting drunk on weekends and sleeping with his girl friend. For a long time I didn't want to believe it, but finally I realized that, if I cared for Dave, I couldn't deny it any longer. As the Bible says, "Faithful are the wounds of a friend . . ." (Proverbs 27:6).

I prayed. Wow, did I ever pray! The more I prayed about what to say, the more scared I got, because I knew I couldn't convince him that he was wrong. After all, who was I to say he was wrong? I myself was no Mr. Clean. I needed a higher authority.

Two verses became like headlights to light my path: The scalpel verse, "For the word of God is living and active, sharper than any two-edged sword, piercing to the division of soul and spirit, of joints and marrow, and discerning the thoughts and intentions of the heart" (Hebrews 4:12). And, "All scripture is inspired by God and profitable for teaching, for reproof, for correction, and for training in righteousness, that the man of God may be complete, equipped for every good work" (2 Timothy 3:16, 17).

I knew it wasn't my own words or my own morals I was to lay on my brother, but God's.

As I went over to his house, picked him up, and we went out for a drive you can be sure I felt no better than he did. After some surface talk, he could tell I was getting nervous. To avoid further awkwardness, I quit beating around the bush and decided to take out the scalpel and begin surgery: "Dave, I want to read you some verses from the Bible. If I seem nervous, it's because I have never done anything like this, and I do care about you a lot. Do you mind if I read you these verses?"

He shook his head no. He seemed to know what was coming.

" 'But I say, walk by the Spirit, and do not gratify the desires of the flesh,' " I started. " 'For the desires of the flesh are against the Spirit, and the desires of the Spirit are against the flesh; for these are opposed to each other, to prevent you from doing what you would. . . . Now the works of the flesh are plain: fornication, impurity, licentiousness . . . drunkenness, carousing, and the like. I warn you as I warned you before, that those who do such things shall not inherit the kingdom of God' " (Galatians 5:16, 17, 19, 21).

"Dave," I added, "do you think that you have been doing things that have been motivated by your own evil instincts and desires—some of the things in this list—rather than the things that please God?"

Inside I cringed for asking such a personal question. "Yes, you're right," he admitted. I couldn't believe it. He admitted he was wrong. Then he added, "But I don't see what's wrong with it, I mean, we are in love." Oh, no! That was just what I was afraid of: Dave knew what he was doing contradicted what the Bible said, yet he didn't care to do anything about it.

At that point I shot up a quick dart to God. "Come on, Lord, here I am sitting under this streetlight, feeling like a fool. You told me Your Word was a scalpel—it sure seems like it's got a blunt edge. You've got to do something."

Suddenly a verse popped into my head; "If you love me, you will keep my commandments" (John 14:15). I read it to him and then asked, "Dave, we've known each other a long time—we've worshiped the Lord, prayed, and taught the Bible together. I have always thought that you loved Jesus. Now you tell me that you know what He wants from you, but you don't care because you *love* your girl friend. What about your *love* for Jesus? Whom do you *really love?*"

Apparently, the scalpel did the job. Within minutes we were out of the car, on our knees, praying—confessing sin, repenting from bad habits, making pivotal decisions to change future behavior. As tears fell off both our cheeks, I couldn't help but silently say, "Jesus, the scalpel really does work! Thanks."

Sometimes it hurts to get cut open by the truth. As Mark Twain said, "Most people are bothered by those passages in Scripture which they cannot understand; but as for me, I always noticed that the passages in Scripture which trouble me most are those which I do understand." When our behavior doesn't live up with the Bible, we can be sure there's nothing wrong with the Bible. It's time to change our behavior.

Lousy Readers

When some hear they are supposed to read the Bible, they dismiss the idea by simply saying, "But I don't *like* to read."

I stand as an example of a poor reader who learned to love to read the Bible. As incredible as this may seem, I graduated from high school having read only one book other than the Bible: *Maybe I'll Pitch Forever,* by Leroy "Satchel" Paige. (Obviously, it was not assigned reading.) I didn't like to read, and I was poor at it. I would much rather go swimming or throw a football than sit passively reading some boring book. I was so uninterested in reading, during my high-school years, my mother told me I could stay up as late as I wanted, provided I was reading. She knew that I would fall asleep with a book in my hands.

When I met Jesus, that all changed. Without anyone telling me I should, I started reading the Bible every night, because I wanted to. When my parents noticed that I was skipping my favorite TV shows in order to read the Bible, they knew something strange was happening. Their son had changed. When they found my light on at midnight, they had to change their rule about staying up as late as I wanted. I loved to read the Bible because it was alive—it was exciting. It was filled with things to learn and things to do.

The policy of Bible study I followed was this: *Read until you find something to do.* I have since attended seminary and learned more thorough methods of Bible study, but I have never gotten beyond seeing the Bible as a book to live. Some passages obviously turn me on more than others, and the "drier" sections often kept me up quite late, but I read until I found something to obey. I didn't care how late I had to stay up, because the Bible never let me down. It was always practical, and sooner or later I would find something challenging.

I agree with D. L. Moody: "I know the Bible is inspired, because it inspires me."

If you are a poor reader, remember the key to Bible study is not how much you *read*, but how much you *obey*. Don't burden yourself with goals that are beyond your reach. Just commit yourself to read at a set time every day, until you find something God wants you to do or something you never knew before.

Setting Standards

We have seen a disintegration of standards in our country.

"Who says it's wrong to go all the way?"
"A little grass or cocaine never hurt anyone."
"Abortion? Sure, a woman has the right to control her own body."
"Mom, I don't care what you say. You and dad are just too old-fashioned."

Jesus predicted this moral landslide, "In the last days wickedness will be multiplied and most men's love will grow cold" (*see* Matthew 24:12).

In writing to Timothy, Paul predicted this period of history could make things tough on Christians. It sounds as if it were written yesterday:

> You may as well know this too, Timothy, that in the last days it is going to be very difficult to be a Christian. For people will love only themselves and their money; they will be proud and boastful, sneering at God, disobedient to their parents, ungrateful to them, and thoroughly bad. They will be hardhearted and never give in to others; they will be constant liars and troublemakers and will think nothing of immorality. They will be rough and cruel, and sneer at those who try to be good. They will betray their friends; they will be hotheaded, puffed up with pride, and prefer good times to worshiping God. They will go to church, yes, but they won't really believe anything they hear. Don't be taken in by people like that.
>
> 2 Timothy 3:1–5 TLB

Our society has gone from morality to permissiveness, to immorality, to amorality. Amorality is worse than immorality. Immorality at least says, "There is a moral standard of right and wrong, even though I am not following it." Amorality flatly says, "There is no such thing." Amorality is legalized immorality.

To counteract such permissiveness, Paul told Timothy to build his moral standard of right and wrong according to the Bible: "All scripture is inspired by God and profitable . . ." (2 Timothy 3:16).

As you read the Bible, looking for something to do, applying God's eternal principles to your life, you will be able to live according to a higher standard.

A Healthy Example

I have prayed with many people when they received forgiveness of sins and life eternal from Jesus, but when I prayed with Peter, I wanted to be sure he was not only converted, but *discipled.* I was tired of overseeing the spiritual birth process, only to turn them loose like orphans. I made arrangements to see him the next day and bought him a brand-new study Bible. When I gave it to him, I explained how just as everyone needs to eat to feed his body, so everyone needs to feed his soul with the Word of God—the Bible. I gave him a list of books to read and study-guide questions to ask of each book. "Set aside fifteen minutes every day for prayer and Bible reading," I suggested. He agreed to do the reading and to meet with me every afternoon to compare notes. We prayed together, and I left.

Every day for three weeks we met together. During that time, he read through the following books of the Bible: John; Genesis; Proverbs; 1, 2 Timothy; Revelation; Acts; Mark; 1 Corinthians; Romans; Joshua; 1, 2 Peter; James; Nehemiah; Exodus; Deuteronomy; and Ecclesiastes. That was a lot of food, but he was a growing boy.

Peter kept reading the Bible. His fifteen minutes quickly became thirty minutes and then an hour. In three months he had read all sixty-six books. The exciting part was not just how much he read, but that he put into practice what he was learning. He would frequently phone to tell me what God had spoken to him about and how he was changing his behavior.

(If you want to begin reading through and studying certain books of the Bible, as Peter did, see Appendix C "Bible Study Guide Questions.")

Some Tips

Your Bible should be as personal as an old pair of jeans. You need to be honest with yourself when you read it.

Buy one that feels right to you. Pick it out yourself. Don't worry about the cost; it's the best investment you'll ever make.

Don't treat it too formally, or it will make you feel stiff and fake. Write in it, underline, use stars, exclamation points, with your own comments in the margin. When you don't understand something, put a small question mark next to it. When God really speaks to you, put the date in the margin, indicating that you have either claimed the promise or are willing to obey the command.

While in college I began marking with three different colored pens:

Red—promises
Black—commands
Blue—general information or points of interest

Using this system helps me to interact with what I am reading.

C. T. Studd made it a habit to buy a new Bible every year, because he marked it so thoroughly. Even though it was an added expense, his communication with God was worth it.

Looking back at my collection of old Bibles is interesting and sometimes embarrassing. Not all my comments are very mature, but at least my old Bibles don't look new. After all, "A Bible that is falling apart is usually owned by someone who isn't." If you don't wear out a Bible every year, perhaps you're not reading it enough.

Autobiography

Barry McGuire met Jesus by reading the Bible. Paul Stookey's heart was prepared to meet Jesus by reading the Bible. There is one simple reason for this pattern of discovering Jesus through reading this Book— it's His autobiography!

Jesus said, "You search the scriptures, because you think that in them you have eternal life; and it is they that bear witness to *me*" (John 5:39, *italics mine*).

To worship the Book is idolatry, but failure to worship Him is blasphemy. As His followers we should love to read His book. He inspired its writing, and it's all about Him. If we love Jesus, we'll love the Bible.

Think

1. What keeps people from reading the Bible?
2. What morals taught in the Bible are "old-fash-ioned," according to today's standards?
3. What is the central theme that runs through the whole Bible?
4. Has the Bible ever become a scalpel, convicting you of sin and slicing it out of your life? Give an illustration.
5. Has reading the Bible ever seemed like a "bor-ing drag"? List five things that can help Bible reading be more exciting.

Act

1. If you don't have a Bible you really enjoy read-ing, take thirty dollars to your local Christian bookstore and buy a beauty. (I recommend the New International Version. It's readable and accurate.)
2. If you don't have a set time to read the Bible every day for at least five minutes, start *now.* (Right after you brush your teeth in the morn-ing, after school, or before lights out.) Ask God to help you *not* to miss a single day.
3. It might be helpful to use the "Bible Study Guide Questions" (Appendix C) as you read through various Bible books.
4. Memorize 2 Timothy 3:15, 16 (word perfect) and consider what the Bible is good for.
5. Memorize the titles of the books of the Bible (thirty-nine—Old Testament; twenty-seven—New Testament). It should only take you twenty minutes, and you will never again need to fumble around.

Read

Every young Bible reader should buy Henrietta Mears's *What the Bible Is All About* (Ventura, Calif.: Gospel Light, 1953). It is a gold mine of practical insight into the Word of God.

I hope this chapter becomes a big broom that sweeps all Christians out of our cozy closets or at least slaps us in the face a few times, to wake us up. The closet is no place to live; it's confining, lonely, and stuffy. Jesus wants to knock down the door and help us break through the boldness barrier.

6
Breaking the Boldness Barrier

"Follow me and I will make you become
fishers of men."
Mark 1:17

You show me a kid who doesn't like challenge, and I'll show you a kid who has retired too early. Sometimes the only thing churches give kids to do is erase the blackboards, pass the offering plates, work in the nursery, or sit in the back pew and twiddle thumbs for Jesus. Anyone with half a brain knows there must be more to serving Jesus than that.

The teenagers and young adults whom I know have energy—nuclear generators full of it. They are looking for a place to go—a cause on which to spend it. Jesus says, "Follow me, and I will give you something to spend all that energy on—I will make you fishers of men" (*see* Matthew 4:19).

Plexiglas Shields

The first year of college or high school is often hard. Meeting new kids can easily make us feel insecure. "Will they accept *me?*" Being a Christian even makes it worse: "Will they accept *my Jesus?*" So what we often try to do is to let them get to know us first; then they can get to know about Jesus.

As a freshman in high school, I went out for football and played both offense and defense, and I made friends. As school progressed, I made more friends. Then came the hard part: letting them get to know that I loved Jesus. Every time I tried to tell them by dropping some little clue, it sailed over their heads like a paper airplane. As I sat in church one Sunday night, hearing a rip-snorting message about how I should be out there telling my friends about Jesus, I got convicted and promised the Lord that I would tell someone about Him the next day.

Monday morning I sat in the library, reading *Time* magazine, praying, "Lord, please send someone to sit next to me, whom I can talk with about You." In walked my best friend, and I panicked. "Oh, no, Lord! Surely you don't mean him, Lord! Send me someone else!" There I sat with my eyes stuck on *Time* magazine, and I couldn't even say, "Good morning." I felt as if I had a Plexiglas shield around me; I could see through it but not reach out of it. I was caught in my closet. I felt like a fool.

It was my fault; I had built a reputation around me. People knew me as an athlete, a friendly, normal, well-dressed kid—just the way I wanted them to think. But I successfully kept them from seeing Jesus in me. By my silence I was telling them a lie. Sure, when they asked me what I did over the weekend, I got brave and even included the fact that I went to church, but I never told them anything about personally knowing Jesus.

We are either secular or Christian; we cannot be both at once. Either we are fooling everyone else six days of the week, or we are fooling ourselves on one day. In either case, we are foolish!

When Jesus came into our lives, He came in to harmonize, make us whole and complete, 100 percent under His control. He did not simply add a religiousness to us, but rather came to completely take over, so that "whatever we do, in word or deed, we do everything in the name of the Lord Jesus, giving thanks to God the Father through him" (*see* Colossians 3:17).

We don't always need to wear a Jesus button or put Jesus bumper stickers on our cars (although both have been helpful to me). It is important that we are always conscious that, in everything we do as Christians, Jesus' reputation is at stake. Consider the areas of our lives that affect the way people think of Jesus.

The *friends* we hang around with and the things we do with them
The *language* we use
The *activities*—the movies, the parties, the concerts, the dances and proms
The *clothes* we wear
The way we spend our *money*
The *music* we listen to

We can never say, "I'm an off-duty Christian. Don't pay any attention to me now." People who don't read the Bible read us from cover to cover. And when they hear we are *Christians*, they sure look close.

My Jesus Identity

"In Christ" or "in the Lord" is such an important Christian principle that these expressions are used 164 times in the New Testament books written by Paul. It certainly indicates our legal standing before the Father, having been justified by Jesus' sacrificial death, but it also refers to the self-image we should have as we live day to day in the world.

As Christians there is no hiding the fact that we are "in Christ." It should be obvious. It will be part of our image, our identity, who we are.

Jesus didn't have to tell His disciples, "Go out there and do the best you can to be the light of the world." No way! He said, "You are the light of the world." Light automatically shines. You can't make light darkness unless you remove the light altogether. When Jesus is inside us, there is no way we can keep Him there. He will shine forth.

This is an important lesson for everyone: There is no way to hide the fact that Christ is in your life when He is really there. It's far better to just let Him out naturally.

Out of the Closet

"But I'm afraid of what people think of me," Josh said. "It really bothers me. I know I shouldn't feel this way, but I do, and I don't know what to do about it. It makes me sick that I just have no boldness at all."

Joshua is not alone. He stands in a long train of lockjaw Christians, whose mouths are frozen with fear and who are living under condemning consciences that keep reminding them that things ought to be different. The only difference between Josh and many others is that he is honest enough to admit that his mediocrity is sin.

I gave Joshua a suggestion: "Pick one kid at school you want to see come to know Jesus and begin praying for him. Then invite him to our youth meeting and tell him about Jesus." He liked the idea. A week later he called, all excited, a few hours before the youth meeting was due to start: "I'm bringing my friend—the one I've been praying for! His name is George, and I want you to tell him about Jesus."

He expected me to share his enthusiasm, but he had only done two-thirds of what I told him to do: He prayed, and he invited his friend to the youth meeting. But he missed the most important part—telling him about Jesus.

"Josh, that's great you have invited George to the meeting tonight, and I will be glad to meet him, but I want *you* to tell him about Jesus. I'll pray for you. See you tonight."

That night I made it a point to meet George, but when the meeting was over, I avoided talking to him because I wanted Josh to take the opportunity to tell his friend about Jesus. The next week Josh called again, asking the same thing, "I'm bringing George again tonight. He liked it last week, and he wanted to come back—now don't miss the opportunity again, I want you to share Jesus with him."

I held my ground, "Josh, you don't understand. He's your friend; you are responsible to tell him about Jesus."

"But I don't know as much as you about it!" He started to get mad. "What if I blow it?"

"Josh, what would your coach do if he told you to run a certain pass pattern and you refused, saying, 'No, coach, you run that pattern better than me, you do it! I might drop the ball'?"

"He'd probably cut me from the team," he answered.

"Well, Jesus wouldn't cut you from the team, but He still wants you to learn how to be a witness. After all, it is not your job to lead George to Christ; that's the Holy Spirit's job. All you have to do is tell him how."

That night Josh brought George, and it was the same thing. Josh got uptight and refused to open those locked jaws.

A few days later I got another call from Josh, "Hey, George and I are going golfing; I want you to go with us so you can share Jesus with him while we're playing."

"Joshua!" I was starting to get impatient, "You don't understand! I am not going to tell him the good news; you have to do it. Now you go and do it today, and I will be here praying for you."

Sometime later that afternoon, the phone rang. The voice was so excited I could hardly understand it. Finally I recognized Josh, "Fred, it was fantastic! I brought along a copy of *The Four Spiritual Laws*. Down the first fairway I shared the first law. Down the second fairway I shared the second law; down the third fairway I shared the third law; down the fourth fairway I shared the fourth law; and on the back side of the fourth green we knelt down, and he asked Jesus to forgive his sins and come into his life! I can't believe it! It really happened! It works! The gospel really works!" I could almost see him jumping up and down.

That was only the beginning for Joshua. In the next several weeks he went on to lead thirty-four others to Christ.

Gospel Power

Before you ever become a gospel junkie, you have to believe that the stuff works. That's our problem: We are really not convinced that it has any power. We think maybe there is something wrong with us because we need Jesus. We think no one else is interested in what Jesus has to offer, or maybe, even if they were interested, Jesus might not work for them! How embarrassing that would be!

Paul gave away the secret of his boldness: "For I am not ashamed of the gospel: it is the *power* of God for salvation to every one who has faith, to the Jew first and also to the Greek" (Romans 1:16, *italics mine*). Why wasn't Paul insecure or uneasy talking to people about Jesus? Very simply: He knew it worked! It's powerful!

"Wait Till You Hear What Happened to Me!"

Paul was not ashamed because he knew the power—not just in his head, but in his heart and life. Jesus exploded inside him and radically changed his thinking and his life-style.

We will never share his boldness unless we share his experience. Obviously we don't need the thunderbolt from heaven or the scales dropping dramatically from our eyes, but we sure need something: We need the personal knowledge that *Jesus changed me.*

There are two very different people who were used greatly by God to influence their whole towns because they simply shared what Jesus did for them.

The first is a man who was a social reject. He lived in a cemetery, where he had broken out of the chains placed on him by the townspeople, who were embarrassed by his abnormal behavior. He intentionally cut himself with rocks and cried out in great misery, with a roaring voice like a baboon. When he met Jesus, evil spirits were cast out of him, and he was completely healed of all his physical, spiritual, mental, and emotional problems. He was a new man. He wanted to leave town and live elsewhere (who wouldn't want to get away from a reputation like that!). But the Lord told him to stay where he was. "Go home to your friends, and tell them how much the Lord has done for you . . ." (Mark 5:19) God told him. Then when the townspeople saw the change in his behavior, they, too, came to Christ by the dozens. This man was never trained in a Bible school, nor was he a man of great influence. To the contrary, he was a misfit. But Jesus changed his life, he knew it, and he told people about it, and they gave their lives to Christ. (*See* Mark 5:1–20.)

The second example is a woman who, like many today, lived with several men. She was religious, but certainly not a believer. One afternoon she met Jesus, who, to her surprise, accepted her for who she was, without making her feel condemned and dirty. He pointed out the difference between being religious and being a genuine Christian, and she was glad to put her faith in Him and be forgiven. Her life was so changed that she started telling all her friends and neighbors about Jesus, and they, too, believed in Him because of her testimony. In fact, they said, "It is no longer because of your words that we believe, for we have heard for ourselves, and we know this is indeed the Savior of the world." (*See* John 4:7–42).

There is power in telling others what Jesus has done for us. Rather than immediately saying, "Here's what Jesus wants to do for *you*," we can say, "Here's what He did for *me*." Not everyone will accept what we say, but it is hard for them to argue with what happened to us. If we say, "I like strawberry ice cream," they can't say, "No, you don't." And if we say, "I know where we can get some, would you like to go?" they might decline, but there is no offense or hostility. They might even say, "Sure. Where to?"

Starting Somewhere

Breaking the ice is always the hardest part, especially when it has had a long time to freeze up. When one has already built a reputation as either a non-Christian or a nonaggressive lockjaw Christian, it is hard to break loose.

Joshua started by inviting a friend to a youth meeting. That at least made it public that he was "religious," but he learned that was not enough. When he started talking about his relationship with Jesus, the massive wall of ice crumbled. His jaw got unlocked, and he zealously (some might say fanatically) shared his faith with almost all his friends. The tool that helped him get started was *The Four Spiritual Laws.* (This can be bought at most Christian bookstores or directly from Campus Crusade.)

The ice breaker for me was carrying my Bible to school. Being a coward, I would never have carried my big, leather Bible, but I was given a paperback that looked like any other paperback. When I started reading that in the library, my friends who had never seen me read anything other than *Time* magazine asked what it was. When they found out it was a Bible, it didn't seem to bother them. In fact frequently they would ask to borrow it. I would point out some interesting verses and then ask them what they thought of Jesus.

I know of another student who got the birthdates of every classmate and sent each a birthday card, including a personal note about his relationship with Jesus.

There are thousands of approaches, but there is *one* especially designed for you. You need to ask Jesus on your own for a method that is best for you. You can be assured He has one in mind. (*See* Appendix E: Nine Icebreakers)

Bringing to a Decision

By the time I was a senior, I had not seen any of my friends come to Christ, even though they all knew that I was a Christian. I had told most of them about me and Jesus, but I needed to appeal to them directly about their relationship with Him. I prayed and asked God to give me an opening—something to say to break the ice. Finally I got a good idea: "I have known you for a long time. You are one of my best friends, yet I have never told you personally about the most important thing in my life. Would you mind if I told you?" It was honest and to the point.

I called Dave and asked him to come over because I wanted to talk with him about something very important. He came right over. I was scared. I can still remember seeing his van pull up to our house. I didn't want my parents to hear me, so I ran out, sat him down in the van, and said, "Dave, you and I are good friends, yet I have never told you about the most important thing in my life. Would you mind if I told you about it right now?" He agreed. (How could he say no?)

I read him a few verses from the Bible, told him how I met Jesus, and asked him if he wanted to do the same. We talked for a while and then knelt there in his van, and he asked Jesus to forgive his sins and come into his life. Wow! I couldn't believe it! This thing of sharing the gospel really worked!

I used that same method with other friends who have also prayed with me to receive Christ. Openings are so important. We know what to say once we get started, but first we need to break the ice. Once the ice is broken, we need to bring them to the point of decision. The results are God's responsibility, but communicating the message is our job.

> I simply argue that the cross be raised again
> at the center of the marketplace
> as well as on the steeple of the church.
> I am rediscovering the claim that
> Jesus was not crucified in a cathedral
> between two candles
> but on a cross between two thieves;
> on the town garbage heap,
> at a crossroad so cosmopolitan
> that they had to write His title
> in Latin and in Hebrew and in Greek.
> At the kind of place where cynics talk smut
> and thieves curse and soldiers gamble;
> Because that is where He died
> and that is what He died about
> and that is where Christians ought to be
> and what Christians ought to be about.
>
> GEORGE MCLEOD

Reprinted by permission of *Jubilee* (May 1979), monthly newsletter of Prison Fellowship.

Think

1. Are you ever embarrassed to tell your friends about Jesus? Why?
2. If you were on trial for being a Christian, with your friends as the witnesses, what evidence would there be to convict you?
3. Have you ever prayed with someone to receive Christ?
4. What are some tips that have been helpful to you in telling others about Jesus?

Act

1. One of the most helpful tools in telling others about Jesus is *The Four Spiritual Laws* (Arrowhead Springs, Calif.: Campus Crusade). Buy a pack, read through one yourself, and then read through it with a friend.
2. Take three pages of notebook paper and write out your personal story of how you met Jesus and what He has done in your life. On page one write out what it was like before you met Jesus; on page two write out actually how you received Christ; and on page three write out what it has been like since. (Write it from the perspective of reading it in front of the student body at your graduation.)
3. Make a list of three friends (or close family members) who have not yet received Christ. Begin praying daily for them and seek to share the gospel with them.
4. Look through Appendix E: Nine Icebreakers. Pick an *opening line* to begin talking with a friend about Jesus, call him or her up today, and get your feet wet.

5. Memorize Romans 1:16 (word perfect) and make it your goal this year.

Read

1. Another book I wrote that will be helpful to you as you seek to break the boldness barrier is *Dare to Be Different* (Old Tappan, N.J.: Fleming H. Revell Co., 1980).
2. I would also strongly recommend the following: Dr. James Kennedy, *Evangelism Explosion* (Wheaton, Ill.: Tyndale House Publishers); Paul Little, *How to Give Away Your Faith* (Wheaton, Ill.: Inter-Varsity Press); Rebecca Manley Pippert, *Out of the Saltshaker: Evangelism as a Way of Life* (Wheaton, Ill.: Inter-Varsity Press, 1979).

7
Taking It on the Chops

"... A servant is not greater than his master. If they persecuted me they will persecute you, if they kept my word, they will keep yours also."
John 15:20

It is common knowledge that if we follow Jesus the way we should and publicly tell others about Him, we will at least be misunderstood and possibly even lose certain friends. This is why Jesus never promised us smooth sailing. He made it clear there would be times when we would take it on the chops.

Persecution in the Classroom

Not long ago my phone rang. It was Barbara. "What's wrong?" I could tell by her voice she had been crying.

"Fred, I feel like such a failure." She explained, "You see, I took your books to school, and I was reading them in the study hall. First, the girl in front of me borrowed one; then the two girls on either side borrowed the others. When they started asking me all sorts of questions about God and heaven and my faith, I started to get all excited. The teacher told us to be quiet, but they kept talking about what they were reading. Finally the teacher came over—oh, Fred. . . ."

She cried and then continued.

"He read the titles out loud and teased me, asking me to tell him where some Bible verse was found, which I didn't know. So everyone laughed at me, and he told me I couldn't be a Christian, since I didn't know the reference. When he sat down, they teased me, and they all threw the books at me and called me names. It was awful."

It sounded awful, and I could feel her hurt, but she wasn't through yet.

"I tried to pray, but I couldn't, so I wrote out a prayer on a piece of paper. Then the teacher came over and read the prayer I had written— out loud to the whole class. I just felt terrible: I wanted to crawl out the window. Oh, Fred, what do I do? Did I blow it?"

"Barb, you now know better than before what it means to follow Jesus." Then I read her these words of Jesus, " 'Blessed are you when men revile you and persecute you and utter all kinds of evil against you falsely on my account. Rejoice and be glad, for your reward is great in heaven, for so men persecuted the prophets who were before you' " (Matthew 5:11, 12). And I added, "In some special way I know God will honor you for this. Just think, you might have been the only high-school kid in the state of Florida today to get mocked for following Jesus."

I don't think she was impressed with my sermonette. She was hurt. But she hung in there. She didn't fully understand what was happening, but she trusted God to work things out.

Four weeks ago one of the friends who laughed at Barb in the study hall came to church with her. That morning she prayed with Barb and gave her life to Jesus. Perhaps Barb lost a few temporary friends, but at least one girl will be in heaven for all eternity.

Sure it's risky to follow Jesus, but it is the only way to live.

The Fear of Man

There are basically three types of reputation: a good reputation, a bad reputation, or no reputation at all (blah!). Any of these can cause a constant fear of rejection.

The Rocky III syndrome—fearing that one might not always be the champ—eats away at many young people. To be the star athlete, star student, or favorite child can be a heavy burden, especially when everyone is cheering, "You can do it!" and inside you're saying, "Will you still like me, if I don't?"

As I am writing this, I am at a high-school camp in central Florida. A girl pulled me aside after breakfast, with tears in her eyes, asking if we could talk. "I'm tired of it, Fred. It's hard to always have everyone looking at me, saying, 'You can do it!' On the softball team and the debating team and even at home my parents think I can do no wrong. My mother keeps telling me I am an example for everyone else. I feel as if I need a vacation from life, just to step out of the spotlight so I can be *me*." After a little talk she saw that even though she was a Christian, her focus shifted from serving Jesus to serving her good reputation.

Chris Evert Lloyd explains that she has to deal with this on the tennis court:

I'm sensitive about how people judge me. It's not so much whether they like me or not; I only ask to be treated fairly. Judge me as I am, not how you think I am. I'm not cold and indifferent. I project cool on the court because my game demands my total commitment. You can't stand at the baseline and gut out and lay rally against a tough opponent when visions of a boy friend dance through your head or you're trying to placate the public and press with gestures, trick shots and plastic smiles.

When you stand at the top of the pile, many eyes are on you, and it's hard not to look at yourself.

Fear of Being Locked Into a Bad Reputation

The worst reputation is no reputation at all. Some kids do the most drugs or drink the most beer or go to bed with the most girls just to have a reputation at something.

In either case—fear of losing a good reputation or fear of being locked into a bad reputation—there is fear that must be dealt with.

As the Bible says, "The fear of man lays a snare . . ." (Proverbs 29:25). If we make it our goal to avoid hostility and misunderstanding at any cost, we will never follow Jesus as we should. But if we intend to tell others about Jesus, we need to break out of the snare and not be afraid to take it on the chops.

Giving Your Reputation to God

There is one way to rid ourselves of the fear of losing our reputations, and that is to give our reputations to God. After all, no one can steal from you what you have already given away. If you give God your reputation right now, you won't need to worry about anyone taking it from you in the future.

Roger came up to me after a Bible study, "Fred, I really want to be a witness, but I am afraid of what people will think of me. I mean, they don't think too much of me right now. I just don't think I could handle any further rejection."

I told him about giving his reputation to Jesus and trusting Him with it. He agreed, so we got on our knees, and he gave it over: "Lord, I trust You with what people think of me. There are times when they don't think too much of me, but even if they reject me completely, I trust You with it. I just want to obey You by telling them about Your love. So I give You my reputation. Please take good care of it."

Three weeks later Roger was riding home on the school bus. His Bible was on top of his other books, and one of the kids knocked it on the floor. Then after another, kids started teasing him, slapping him, and calling him names: *fanatic, weirdo, Joe Christian.* He got off the bus and walked home, feeling as if he had lost a war. While shooting baskets, trying not to lick the wounds, the phone rang. Phil, one of the kids on the bus, wanted to come over and talk with him.

"Roger, you must really believe in the Bible and in this man Jesus to stand up under all that criticism. How can I know Jesus the way you know Him?" They opened Roger's Bible, and that afternoon Phil asked Jesus into his heart.

Roger realized, *Wow, what a small price; I risked my temporal reputation for his eternal soul.*

We sure can be selfish; we are afraid people might reject us if we tell them about Jesus, while it doesn't bother us to know they are going to hell without Him.

When we meet Jesus, He turns us inside out. We no longer think only of ourselves, but we are more concerned about others. We can't possibly let people be damned eternally simply because we can't trust Jesus with our temporal reputations.

Strong Arms

The underlying question is, "Can I trust God to take good care of my reputation?" Let's face it: What our friends think of us is pretty important, and we want to be sure that God has our best interests in mind.

Jesus said, "If you confess me before men, I will confess you before my Father who is in heaven; but if you deny me before men, I will deny you before my Father who is in heaven" (*see* Matthew 10:32, 33).

Has that ever struck you as being a little harsh? I always thought it was harsh, until I saw the context: Jesus was telling His disciples that if they could trust Him with their eternal souls, they could certainly trust Him with their temporal reputations. He also spoke about the fear of man:

"And do not fear those who can kill the body" (*see* Matthew 10:28). If they feared God, all other fears should evaporate.

This hits right at the heart of faith.

Do I really believe that God loves me?
Do I believe that He is powerful enough to protect me?
While I say I trust Him with my soul, can I also trust Him with my reputation?
Does He really have my best interests in mind?
Can I do what He tells me and still enjoy life?

We either believe it, or we don't. Either we are convinced that we can throw ourselves without reserve into the strong arms of God's love, or we just can't trust Him at all.

Barb and Roger threw themselves into God's strong arms, and they held. Listen to this description of those mighty arms (Romans 8:31, 32, 37–39):

. . . If God is for us, who is against us?
He who did not spare his own Son but gave him up for us all, will he not also give us all things with him?
. . . In all . . . things we are more than conquerors. . . .
For I am sure that neither death, nor life, nor angels, nor principalities, nor things present, nor things to come, . . . nor height, nor depth, nor anything else in all creation, will be able to separate us from the love of God in Christ Jesus our Lord.

The Badge of Commitment

Being killed for Jesus might sound to you like an impossibility, but in a few years it might not seem so impossible. What will you do then?

In the early church, martyrdom (getting killed because of one's faith in Jesus) was always a possibility; so much so that the Greek word for "to witness" is the same as the word *martyr*. In Acts 1:8 (*italics mine*) we read, "But you shall receive power when the Holy Spirit has come upon you; and you shall be my *witnesses* [Greek word: *martures*]. . . ."

There is no higher badge of commitment than dying for your faith.

This is a badge Jesus expects every disciple to be willing to wear. We can't say, "Aw, that's okay for the supersaints like Stephen or Peter or Jim Elliot. But God would never expect that from me."

We could well be members of the final generation of Christians. If we are, we will face increasing opposition from our secular society. The warfare is going to intensify. Even today, over 60 percent of the Christians on this planet live in countries where they suffer severe persecution.

Just think about this verse, "And they have conquered him by the blood of the Lamb and by the word of their testimony, for they loved not their lives even unto death" (Revelation 12:11). This verse vividly describes the warfare we have with the devil. Clearly it is the blood of Jesus that conquered Satan. However the sign that His blood has *worked* in us is that it makes us willing to lay down our lives for Him—to love not our own lives even unto death. This is the badge of a Christian—every Christian—because, when the love that led Jesus to lay down His life for us on the cross genuinely lays hold of us, we will willingly lay down our lives for Him.

Someone has said, "It is easier to die for Him than it is to live for Him." But it is also easier to live for Him once you have agreed to die for Him. Those who make such a commitment are not *supersaints;* they are *simply saints.* Every saint needs to know that is part of the cost of commitment. Total commitment or no commitment: That is the decision we face.

Think

1. Have you ever been teased or discriminated against for being a follower of Christ? What did it feel like?
2. "The fear of man lays a snare ..." (Proverbs 29:25). Describe in your own words "The fear of man." Have you experienced it? Explain.
3. What does it mean to give your reputation to God?
4. Think hard: Would you be willing to die for Jesus?
5. "Total commitment or no commitment." Do you agree or disagree?

Act

Memorize 1 Peter 4:14 (word perfect). It will come in handy when you take it on the chops.

8
Declaring War

"Praise the Lord and pass the
ammunition."
Chaplain Howell M. Forgy
Pearl Harbor

A few years ago I took a busload of kids to a Barry McGuire concert in downtown Boston. I thought that sounded harmless enough. When we walked into the auditorium, I sensed something strange, so I grabbed a Christian friend, and we went down to the basement to pray for Barry and the whole concert. When he walked out on stage, there were untimely shouts and even some heckling, which was odd for a Christian concert. Through the evening people would yell, "Praise the Lord," and "Hallelujah" at awkward moments, and Barry had to tell them to be quiet. Sitting near the front of the auditorium, we could see that Barry was obviously laboring to keep things going. Finally, after only an hour, he asked us to stand for prayer to end the concert. Before he could say the first word of his prayer, someone up on the upper balcony let loose with a screeching voice in an unknown language—a demonic tongue! It sent shivers up my spine, as it was obviously not from God. In seconds, Barry rebuked the evil spirit and told the person to leave and get help. After a brief prayer, McGuire walked off, and we were left looking at one another. Everyone around us was saying, "Wow, what a weird concert!" and "Wasn't that gross?" The busload of kids whom I brought stared at me with big eyes—they looked as if they had been to a horror film.

Oh, no! What am I going to say to their parents when they ask me what kind of concert I took their kids to? I asked myself as we got on the bus. *Man, am I ever in trouble! I'll probably get fired as youth minister.* The bus was dead silent. They were scared stiff.

As I was sitting in the front seat, a kid tapped me on the shoulder, "Fred, Sally is crying in the back of the bus. She's really scared, would you talk to her?"

Well, Lord, maybe You can make something good out of this..., I thought as I walked toward the back.

Sally asked me, "Was that the *devil* talking?" When I told her I thought it was, she said, "Fred, I never realized that the devil was so real before tonight. I have been playing around with my life, not really taking

God seriously, but I sure don't want to be living for the devil. He's gross! Could I pray and give my life over to Jesus?"

After we were done praying, two guys called me over to talk with them. "We have been talking, and we want to give our lives to Jesus. For the first time, we realize that you are either for God or you're for the devil, and there is no way that we want to mess around with Satan."

Those kids never forgot that concert, because for the first time they realized the existence of a personal devil who has supernatural power. Up until then, if you asked them who the devil was, they would say, "Aw, he's just like Santa Claus—he is really your father."

Identify the Enemy

The devil is no one to mess around with. He is our enemy, and of all people in the world, he hates followers of Jesus the most. More than prostitutes, druggies, murderers, and witches, his efforts are being focused against Christians. Just as it would be foolish to fight a war without recognizing the enemy, so God doesn't want us ignorant of our spiritual enemy, who has already declared all-out war.

Just listen to the titles given to this scoundrel:

Enemy (*Satan* literally means "enemy") (1 Peter 5:8)
Tempter (1 Thessalonians 3:5)
Deceiver (2 Corinthians 11:3)
Hinderer (1 Thessalonians 2:18)
Roaring lion (1 Peter 5:8)
God of this world (2 Corinthians 4:4)
Prince of the power of the air (Ephesians 2:2)
A liar and the father of lies (John 8:44)
Slanderer (Greek *diablos*, "devil") (Revelation 12:9)
Accuser of our brethren (Revelation 12:10)
Destroyer (Revelation 9:11)

This same one is called the angel of light because he usually does not parade his weirdness, but hides it behind a beautiful mask (2 Corinthians 11:14).

Just consider some of his main activities:

Murders his own kids (Isaiah 14:20, 21)
Wrestles with all Christians (Ephesians 6:12)
Wars with saints (Revelation 12:17)
Governs over the world system (Ephesians 2:1, 2)
Blinds the spiritual eyes of unbelievers (2 Corinthians 4:4)

Unless you don't believe in God's Word, there is no denying the devil.

This supernatural chump has a host of demons at his command (*see* Ephesians 6:12):

Principalities
Powers
World rulers of this present darkness
Spiritual hosts of wickedness in heavenly places

Apparently, one-third of the angels of yesteryear are currently fallen angels in Satan's service (Revelation 12:3, 4). If the number of angels is placed near 100 million (Revelation 5:11), and if the calculation of one-third can be taken literally, there are at least 30 million malignant spirits spreading spiritual disease on this planet. That is nothing to mess around with.

Satan Hits Hollywood

The occult has been woven into the fabric of our country, not only through tens of thousands of witches, but through nursery rhymes, movie and television ghosts, astrology, and other subtle forms of disguise. Forty percent of all teenagers believe the stars affect their lives, according to a recent Gallup poll. Many believe halfheartedly, and others take it with a grain of salt; but when the devil hit Hollywood, people responded to the big screen with such fascination, even film-makers were surprised. It was like throwing a handful of confetti into a fan: It scattered the dark side of the supernatural into the marketplace.

Rosemary's Baby was the first occult film, with many strange occurrences reported at the various theaters at which it was shown. Many called them coincidence, but Anton Szandor LaVey was doing more than playacting as he starred as the devil. At the same time he was filmed in *Rosemary's Baby* he was establishing the Satanic Church in California. He is the author of the Satanic Bible, which has sold more than a quarter million copies. Everyone who joins his church sells his soul to the devil, and their services are far too perverted to mention.

Every year another movie has followed: *The Exorcist, The Omen, Poltergeist, Friday the 13th.* Such films have put the devil in the headlines, and he has become more popular at the box office than anyone predicted.

It needs to be understood that Christians neither deny the reality of these forms of supernatural power and demonstration nor accept their validity. In his famous *The Screwtape Letters,* C. S. Lewis warns of extremes: "There are two equal and opposite errors into which our race can fall about the devils. One is to disbelieve in their existence. The other is to believe, and to feel excessive and unhealthy interest in them." Right on!

Bear Traps

There are many such bear traps, which have been recently set by the devil to catch young, ignorant Christians. Unfortunately we can't spring them. Neither can I point out all of them, but I can show you what they look like.

Although the creators of Dungeons and Dragons deny it, this game is drenched in the occult, including the practices of casting spells, divination, astral projection, sorcery, clairvoyance, and communication with the dead. Not only are these activities found in the occult, they are found nowhere else but the occult. There are subgames such as The Company of the Dark Brotherhood, The Demon Masters, and The Game of Evil Spirits. *Psychology Today* even revealed how the player often gets overengrossed in his fictitious character, to the point of its becoming a sort of alter ego. Tragically the game is selling over $20 million annually; of its total sales, 26 percent are to fifteen- to seventeen-year-olds and a whopping 46 percent to children ages ten to fourteen.

Listen to what God says, "There shall not be found among you . . . one who interprets omens, or a sorcerer, or one who casts spells, a medium or a spiritist, or one who calls up the dead . . . the Lord your God has not allowed you to do so" (*see* Deuteronomy 18:10, 11, 14). Dungeons and Dragons is forbidden fruit for all followers of Christ.

In condemning these things, God sprays DDT on Ouija boards, seances, astrology, white and black magic, palm reading, levitation, and all other satanic-oriented activity. It all deserves to be thrown into the same toilet and flushed!

Many Christian young people still don't see the connection between drugs and the devil. "A little marijuana never hurt anyone," they argue. "The Bible doesn't say there is anything wrong with it."

Yes, the Bible does say there is something wrong with it. The word translated "sorcery" in the New Testament is the Greek word *pharmakia*, from which we get the word *pharmacy*. Wuest, in his *Word Studies in the Greek New Testament,* volume 1, explains "Witchcraft is from *pharmakia*, which word speaks in general of the use of drugs, whether helpfully by a physician or harmfully by someone whose purpose it is to inflict injury." Apparently, the ancient witches were a bunch of pot heads or opium freaks, who knew that by lowering their level of consciousness through hallucinogens, it was easier to make contact with evil spirits. The use of drugs and witchcraft is included in the list of deeds done by those cast into the lake of fire (Galatians 5:20; Revelation 9:21; 18:2, 3; 22:15).

Remember, what *feels* right is not necessarily what *is* right. Satan is an angel of light. There is a beautiful side of evil that can cause us to lustfully drool, but we must not keep returning, like a dog, to the same old vomit.

Secular rock music is sick. It's like a bloody boxer up against the ropes, waiting for the bell to ring. Even Ted Nugent was quoted in *Rolling Stone* magazine, "I'm bowing to me. There's nothing spiritual about it. It is the total celebration of the physical. It is the ultimate physical statement this side of clubbing your dinner."

It became public knowledge that Led Zeppelin's album, *Stairway to Heaven* contained a song that, when played backwards, said, "I live for Satan," even a few non-Christian kids scratched their heads. (Remember, *Satan* literally means "enemy." They were actually singing, "I live for the enemy!"—yes, the archenemy of the human race.)

All rock music is not of the devil. Fortunately today the world is sitting up and taking notice that we Christians are finally producing some music that goes beyond the candy-coated Lawrence Welk ballads from the fifties. As has happened through history, genuine Holy Spirit revival is always accompanied by a breath of creative hymnology, and today we have much excellent Jesus music.

Rock music is too powerful a medium to be neutral. It is either dominated by the Spirit of our creative God, or it is dominated by the devil. Therefore secular rock music communicating sex, drugs, rebellion, and self-seeking is devilish and has no place on a Christian's stereo.

Burning Boats

When we understand the devil doesn't shoot plastic bullets from toy guns, but that he is playing for keeps, we should take a big gulp and get our lives in order. Any area of our lives that has been exposed to him is ground which he potentially occupies, and that ground needs to be gained back.

When Julius Caesar was gaining victory after victory, he landed at England and had his troops climb the cliffs of Dover. When they reached the top, he had them look back. Much to their surprise, their ships were ablaze with fire. "No retreat," he stated. "Advance and conquer."

It is an important principle of spiritual warfare to burn all ships from the past. To destroy all physical emblems: leftover pot, secular rock albums, occult books, games, immoral paperbacks, and so forth. This is what the believers did in Ephesus:

Many also of those who were now believers came, confessing and divulging their practices. And a number of those who practiced magic arts brought their books together and burned them in the sight of all; and they counted the value of them and found it came to fifty thousand pieces of silver.

Acts 19:18

In today's economy, this value would be more than $2.5 million.

Victory

As Christians we don't have to fight *for* victory; we fight *from* victory.
Jesus has won! In renouncing all devilish activities, we need to plead the
blood of Jesus to deliver us from any lingering bondage.

"I saw Satan fall like lightning from heaven."

Luke 10:18

... Now shall the ruler of this world be cast out.

John 12:31

... The reason the Son of God appeared was to destroy the works of
the devil.

1 John 3:8

He disarmed the principalities and powers and made a public example of them, triumphing over them in him.

Colossians 2:15

Finally, be strong in the Lord and in the strength of his might. Put
on the whole armor of God, that you may be able to stand against
the wiles of the devil.

Ephesians 6:10, 11

For the weapons of our warfare are not worldly but have divine
power to destroy strongholds.

2 Corinthians 10:4

When we renounce evil practices, we fasten our arms firmly to
Christ's, and in His mighty Name—the Name above every name—we
command all other shackles to be loosed. In Christ we are then more
than conquerors. Such bondage to Christ is freedom from all other bondage.

Warfare Conditions

During wartime, people learn to live without many things. The luxuries we once considered so important are no longer needed because we

are suddenly concerned with something far more important—staying alive.

The *Queen Mary*, still remembered as a great luxury liner, is now docked in the harbor at Long Beach, California. It floats with a partition down the middle as an illustration of the difference between the peacetime luxuries and the wartime austerities. What a contrast in life-styles!

Prior to World War II, the ship, measuring the length of three football fields, was a luxury liner with elegant dining and large estate rooms providing every imaginable extravagance for a fortunate few who could pay the high prices. When the United States declared war, the ocean liner was converted into a troop transport. The crystal chandeliers and private tables were taken out of the dining rooms, and they became cafeterias, with metal trays with indentations rather than plates and saucers. The spacious private rooms were filled with bunk tiers eight levels high. Rather than holding a comfortable 3,000, as in peacetime, it held 15,000 in wartime.

Such a change in the ship might have been offensive to the peacetime shipmasters, but the survival of our nation depended on it. It was a national emergency. We all had to sacrifice in order to preserve the higher good of peace and security. An ocean luxury liner isn't much good if we are all prisoners of war.

It is time to recognize that we are in a war and that we need to start living under wartime conditions. We need to convert our luxury-liner living into simpler life-styles. Rather than making it our goal in life to get rich or famous, we need to realize that Jesus has commissioned us into His service.

He has enlisted us: "You did not choose me, but I chose you and appointed you that you should go and bear fruit and that your fruit should abide; so that whatever you ask the Father in my name, he may give it to you" (John 15:16).
He clearly describes the enemy: Ephesians 6:11, 12.
He gave us the weapons and the artillery: Acts 1:8; Ephesians 6:12–17.
He gave us the assignment: "Go therefore and make disciples of all nations . . ." (Matthew 28:19).

The problem is we keep going AWOL (absent without leave). We don't understand the important principle of warfare pointed out by Commanding General Paul, "No soldier on service gets entangled in civilian pursuits, since his aim is to satisfy the one who enlisted him" (2 Timothy 2:4).

A Model

There is one overriding characteristic of wartime: We become people of one purpose. When we face life-and-death issues, all the other distracting delicacies of life lose their appeal. Mediocrity is no longer a question; when your existence depends on it, you give everything you've got.

Jim Elliot attended Wheaton College, where he sought to live a consecrated life. At twenty years of age he prayed, "Lord, make my way prosperous, not that I achieve high station, but that my life may be an exhibit to the value of knowing God." There were many good things he avoided because he sought to maintain a singleness of mind. He knew he was heading for the missionary field, so he ate food that would strengthen his body—fresh fruits, raw vegetables, and very few starches and desserts. He was on the wrestling team and stayed physically fit, also thinking of his missionary career.

Jim woke up with enough time before classes to meet with the Lord in Bible study and prayer. "None of it gets to be 'old stuff,' for it is Christ in print, the Living Word." He wrote. "We wouldn't think of rising in the morning without a face wash, but we often neglect that purgative cleansing of the Word of the Lord. It wakes us up to our responsibility." More than academic success, Jim was studying for the AUG degree (approved unto God).

Young Elliot made it a practice of staying in on Saturday night, so he would be alert for worshiping Jesus Sunday morning. Even though it hurt his social life and he had few dates, he was more interested in his romance with Christ.

Besides his disciplined Bible study, he wanted to pray as he ought:

I lack the fervency, vitality, life in prayer which I long for. I know that many consider it fanaticism when they hear anything which does not conform to the conventional, sleep-inducing eulogies so often rising from Laodicean lips; but I know that these same people can . . . tolerate sin in their lives and in the church without so much as tilting one hair of their eyebrows. Cold prayers, like cold suitors, are seldom effective in their aims.

Jim Elliot's passion for God is clearly seen in this prayer:

"He makes His minister a flame of fire." Am I ignitable? God deliver me from the dread asbestos of "other things." Saturate me with the oil of the Spirit that I may be aflame. But flame is transient, often short-lived. Canst thou bear this, my soul—short life? In me there dwells the Spirit of the Great Short-Lived, whose zeal for God's house consumed Him. And He has promised baptism with the Spirit and with Fire. "Make me Thy Fuel, Flame of God."

He was a man of one thing and allowed no distractions to detour his destiny. He added up the facts.

1700 languages have not a word of the Bible translated.
90% of the people who volunteer for the mission field never get there. It takes more than a "Lord I'm willing."
64% of the world have never heard of Christ.
5000 people die every hour.
There is one Christian worker for every 50,000 people in foreign lands, while there is one to every 500 in the United States.
Jesus said, "Go and make disciples of all nations."

Frustrated over the scarcity of missionaries, he said, "Our young men are going into the professional fields because they don't 'feel called' to the mission field. We don't need a call; we need a kick in the pants."

His own life decision is summed up in the words he wrote in 1949, while a college student: "He is no fool who gives what he cannot keep to gain what he cannot lose." Seven years later he was murdered by the Auca Indian tribespeople he was seeking to reach with the message of salvation. Jim gave all he had to the One who gave all He had. Young Elliot saw the battle and was not satisfied to watch from the sidelines. He got down off the bleachers, onto the field, where Jesus is.

Who will take his place among the fighting troops? Jesus has too many spectators. He calls us to take up our arms and fight.

Singleness of Purpose

The single-mindedness of commitment that Jesus had and that He expects His followers to exhibit is sensitively communicated by this poem, written by a girl describing the kind of man she hoped to marry:

> Dear God, I prayed, all unafraid
> (as we're inclined to do)
> I do not need a handsome man
> but let him be like You;
> I do not need one big and strong
> nor yet so very tall,
> nor need he be some genius,
> or wealthy, Lord, at all;
> but let his head be high, dear God,
> and let his eye be clear,
> his shoulders straight, whate'er his state,
> whate'er his earthly sphere;
> and let his face have character,
> a ruggedness of soul,
> and let his whole life show, dear God,
> a singleness of goal;
> then when he comes
> (as he will come)
> with quiet eyes aglow,
> I'll understand that he's the man
> I prayed for long ago.
>
> RUTH BELL GRAHAM

This girl, Ruth Bell, married a man who fit the description: his name, William Franklin Graham, the world's most influential evangelist.

As young men and young women we want to set our sights high, but they must be focused on the single goal of Christ's glory in His eternal dominion. We know who will win the war, but who will stand in battle and claim the victory? Will you?

Think

1. In your own words define *demon, Satan, evil.*
2. Do you really think they exist today? Why?
3. What is Satan's ultimate goal? Will he succeed?
4. Do you think it is wise for a Christian to attend demon-oriented films? Why or why not?
5. List some of the bear traps Satan has set in our society to catch innocent prey.
6. List some wartime characteristics that should also be found in the lives of Christians.

Act

1. In the early church, when people met Jesus, they burned all traces of satanic influence, including books on astrology, black magic, white magic, and so forth (*see* Acts 19:18, 19). If you have any bear traps on your bookshelf, in your drawers or closet, you too need to burn them. These include drug paraphernalia, pornography, horoscopes, and demonic games.
2. Memorize Ephesians 6:10–18. It might save your life.

Read

If Jim Elliot's life sounds exciting, get these two action-packed books on his life, Elisabeth Elliot, *Through Gates of Splendor* (Wheaton, Ill.: Tyndale House, 1981) and *Shadow of the Almighty* (New York: Harper & Row, 1979).

9
When the Roses Wilt

Count it all joy, my brethren, when
you meet various trials, for you know
that the testing of your faith produces
steadfastness.
James 1:2

Every once in a while you hear a story like the one I read in the paper this morning. Emily seemed to have everything to live for: almost straight A's in school, talent in both music and science. Her own parents had high hopes for her. No one could figure out why she went outside before sunup, removed a revolver from her dad's Mercedes, and fired a bullet through her brain. When her parents found a note on the refrigerator, "Love ya, Em," they looked out the window and saw her slumped, struggling for breath. The medical examiner's office ruled it death by suicide.

One teenager attempts suicide in our country almost every minute, yet some people still don't understand that kids hurt. Suicides are always surrounded by dozens of questions, but when an intelligent and talented fourteen-year-old-girl like the one I read about decides she's had enough, there are thousands of unanswered questions. Regardless of what else psychologists try to pin it on, that girl hurt. Her pain pushed her so far that she decided death was preferable to suffering, so she put herself out of her misery.

We don't know the cause of her pain, but that doesn't matter. The fact is, she hurt. Every kid stands in at least part of her shadow. We all get hurt, disappointed and abused, yet as followers of Jesus, we need to learn how to handle it. Most of us have already made the unpleasant discovery that Christians also have problems. We all need to know what to do when the roses wilt.

A Good Teacher

Jesus can teach us how to handle pain because He had to learn how to handle more than His share. Suffering was such a part of His life that He is called a "... man of sorrows, and acquainted with grief..." (Isaiah 53:3). Therefore, when we suffer, Jesus can comfort us, since He knows what it feels like to:

Have the crowd turn against Him
Lose His closest friends
Get mocked and teased
Stand alone
Apparently get cut off from His Father's love
Get stabbed and whipped and nailed to a tree
Feel loneliness, rejection, stress, and futility

Yes, emotionally, socially, mentally, spiritually, and physically, Jesus has felt everything you have ever felt—and then some.

It was no accident that Jesus called His followers disciples. *Discipline* is at the heart of the Christian life. Elsewhere we have dealt with self-discipline—submitting to restrictions and guidelines that we choose for ourselves. Trials and hard times are also discipline, but they are circumstances that are thrown at us against our grain.

The Discipline of Authority

Until we learn to respond properly to authority, we are of no use to God.

Why? Very simply, ". . . There is no authority except from God, and those that exist have been instituted by God" (Romans 13:1). Therefore, to reject authority is to reject God.

There are all sorts of authority:

Civil authority: police, teachers, political leaders
Family: moms, dads, even grandparents
Church: pastors, elders
Employer: boss

All these find their authority delegated by God.

The problems start when they make demands that we either don't agree with or else just don't want to follow. Those problems seem to usually start at home.

Dear Old Dad and Mom

Last week I surveyed 150 teenagers, asking them, "Over what areas do you argue with your parents?" Here's a list they all agreed on:

Friends
Curfew
Classwork
Music (style and volume)
Clothes
Dating
Chores
Spending money
Car
Eating (junk food)
Attitudes
Brothers and sisters

The argument goes this way, "Aw, dad, come on, you just don't understand. I want to make that decision. I am old enough to do what I want."

We hear so much about rights—equal rights, women's rights, civil rights, children's rights—that we think we should demand rights from our parents. Such logic sounds right, but is dead wrong. God wants to teach His children to *yield rights,* and then, when we are able to handle them, He will give them back to us as *responsibilities.*

My dad was strict. He insisted on a ten o'clock curfew, even after I had my driver's license. I can still remember pulling in the driveway after an exciting Bible study where I had led a girl to Christ—it was 10:30 P.M. My dad greeted me at the door without his usual smile. I knew he was mad, but I figured when he heard what I had been doing, it would make a difference. He was not impressed with my story, and since I had not called to tell him I'd be late, I was on restriction.

What a drag! I thought. *It's not fair.* But God was teaching me a lesson without which I would still be a useless servant. During my junior year of high school, God used my father to break me of rebellion, and He taught me to love authority because, ultimately, it all came from Him. By my senior year of high school, my father gave me the responsibility of coming in when I wanted. He gave it only after I was willing to do without it.

Not a Matter of Right or Wrong

We can spit and scrape and kick and holler against God's authorities, screaming, "But, it's just not fair! I am *right* and they are *wrong!*" but we miss the issue. When a God-given authority is involved, it is not a matter of who is right or who is wrong; it's a matter of who is in charge.

When I was twenty I was asked to speak at a statewide teen camp. I knew they had strict dress and grooming standards, which I had agreed to go along with, not because I agreed with them, but because I felt God had asked me to preach the gospel there. Before arriving, I cut my hair at least three inches, so as to not make waves. I no sooner got out of my car than I found myself in the camp director's office, being told to cut my hair or leave: "Above the ear, not touching the ear; above the collar, not touching the collar; above the eyebrows, not touching the eyebrows." It was like being taken out behind the woodshed and scolded.

As much as I dislike confessing this, my heart was furious. *What's the big deal with hair?* I questioned. *Man, my father doesn't even get that strict! Maybe I don't belong here, if they can't accept me the way I am.* On and on my mind rambled and rebelled. I told the man I needed fifteen minutes to think about it, to which he agreed.

Walking off by myself, I talked to Jesus, "What should I do?" I asked. Suddenly it was as if I was back in eleventh grade, having learned nothing about authority: "Get it cut, you butterball!" God seemed to thunder. "Don't you yet understand there are more important things in My Kingdom than *hair?*" Then I heard the words that cut the deepest, "It is not a matter of who is right or who is wrong. It is a matter of *pride!* Your sinful self doesn't want to bow to authority!"

When God was done with me behind the woodshed, all my bologna had been sliced off and was piled high around me. It was a matter of my will against God's appointed authority. That's all I needed. A few minutes later I was walking into the camp director's office, asking him if my hair was short enough, "Sir."

God says, "Likewise you that are younger be subject to the elders.

Clothe yourselves, all of you, with humility toward one another, for 'God opposes the proud, but gives grace to the humble.' Humble yourselves therefore under the mighty hand of God [that's our part], that in due time He may exalt you [that's His part]" (1 Peter 5:5, 6). Until we learn to submit to God's appointed authority over us, He will never exalt us.

Yield Right of Way

Does God have anyone in authority over you, whom you don't like. A non-Christian parent? An unreasonable parent? A boss you don't see eye-to-eye with? Jesus wants you to know that person has been hand-picked by His Father. You need to joyfully submit to that person, even when you disagree with him. In fact every time you don't submit, you lose an opportunity to become like Jesus, and you become stunted in your spiritual development.

Here's the principle:

Your attitude should be the kind that was shown us by Jesus Christ, who, though he was God, did not demand and cling to his rights as God, but laid aside his mighty power and glory, taking the disguise of a slave and becoming like men. And he humbled himself even further, going as far as actually to die a criminal's death on a cross.

Philippians 2:5–8 TLB

Jesus could have enjoyed all the benefits of being God: having the angels wait on Him hand and foot, being worshiped and praised. But He gave up all those rights as God and deliberately chose to humble Himself by becoming a man, a slave, and eventually being sentenced to a criminal's death. Now that is the ultimate in being taken advantage of! He gave up His rights.

When our authorities—especially our parents—ask us to do something that we don't want to do, we have just identified a right that God wants us, as His followers, to give up.

Giving up rights always hurts; it offends our egos and our pride. But don't forget we are followers of the One who said, "If any man would come after me, let him deny himself and take up his cross and follow me" (Matthew 16:24).

An Example

Ruth was the first one in her family to meet Jesus. Her life was changed, and she wanted her parents to see the difference, especially since she had been rebellious and messed up, disappointing her parents greatly. There were, however, some things in her past she had not told her parents—about living with a guy and getting an abortion. They now stood between herself and her parents, so she had to confess them. *What will they think? Here I am a Christian, and I have caused them enough pain!* she thought.

Despite her hesitations, Ruth confessed to them. Her mother cried hard, "How could you do this to me?" Ruth went to her room, wishing she were dead.

Two hours later her mother came in, "Ruth, I know it was harder for you to admit those things than it was for me to hear them. I know that you told us because your life is changed. Can I meet this Jesus, too?"

Late that night Ruth prayed with her mother to receive Christ. She had so wanted to submit to their authority that she even confessed to them her times of insubordination. Because she so humbled herself, God exalted her and allowed her to have the joy of leading her mother to Christ.

Will you allow the cross to sink that deep into your heart? Submitting to authority is not a matter of who's right or wrong; it's a matter of the will—a matter of pride.

The Discipline of Disappointment

Just as it is vital for us to learn how to joyfully submit to those in authority, we need to learn how to respond to situations that seem to go bad. This, too, is discipline.

Disappointments usually involve a loss:

Losing a job
Losing a starting position on the team
Losing a parent through divorce or death
Losing a friend
Losing self-respect

The situations and circumstances of life can turn Jesus' disciples into fair-weather friends. When the weather is fine, we are glad to follow Him. When the weather gets bad, we tend to run for cover. But God doesn't want us to be thermometers; we can be thermostats.

Michelle was only eight when she learned she was going to lose her leg to cancer. When I met her at fourteen, I was amazed to see all she could do: play volleyball, softball, and even go white-water rafting with the rest of her friends. I learned that she skateboards, downhill skis at up to sixty miles per hour, horseback rides, and has won countless awards and prizes for her accomplishments.

After watching her for a few days, I asked her some personal questions:

"Do you ever feel sorry for yourself?"
[Without a moment's hesitation] "No! Why should I?"
"Don't you feel handicapped?"
"No, not really. *Handicapped* is a state of mind, I think. How can any child of God consider himself *handicapped?* I really consider myself very fortunate; I can do a lot of things other people can't do."

There was no question about it; Michelle does more on one leg than most do on two legs. She has so learned to handle her limitations that she feels no embarrassment at all.

When she first came out of the hospital, she asked her dad to walk down the block in her neighborhood. He agreed, so she hobbled along on her new crutches. The neighbors felt so awkward they disappeared into their houses. Without comment, she and her dad kept walking. When they got back inside she suggested the next evening they go door to door, telling each neighbor exactly what happened, to let them know that she was still the same girl they used to know. (That idea came from an eight-year-old!) Her idea worked, and the ice was broken.

Today Michelle is a vibrant, maturing Christian young woman who radiates Jesus because she didn't harbor her handicap, but kept her heart open to God's love, and His love brought her through a hard time.

Kid's Stuff

Unfortunately the hard times often make God seem as if He is against us. These are the times, above all others, when we need to know He is *for* us. God doesn't cause the hard times, but He is *in* the hard times. If we lose sight of that, we are in trouble.

Joseph is a classic example of a young man who kept his eyes on God while he was hurting. He had everything going for him: wealthy parents, brains, skills, influence. The problem was he had brothers—eleven of them—who thought he was a stuck-up creep. They beat him up, threw him in a warehouse, and finally sold him into slavery.

Joseph worked hard to gain an important position as housekeeper in a palace in Egypt, but when the lady of the house tried to go to bed with him, he refused, hurting her pride. She had him put in prison, where he sat with the rats and roaches for several years. Even his friends forgot about him. The whole time, he never grumbled, but kept praising the Lord. Finally, after giving good advice to the king, he was given the exalted position of prime minister.

More than a rags-to-riches story, the account of Joseph climaxed when he finally met up with his brothers toward the end of his life. He could have had them killed, whipped, or at least begging for forgiveness on their knees. Rather Joseph broke down and wept, telling them, "You meant it for evil but God meant it for good." (*See* Genesis 37–50; 50:20.) No bitterness, no resentment, no complaints, just thanksgiving to God for all things.

Joseph knew that no person, no circumstance, no nation, no philosophy, nothing was bigger than God who held his life. Joseph kept his eyes on his heavenly Father, who sovereignly controlled the events that would have sent most people into a tailspin.

If you are in the middle of a brutal situation, know that your Father is bigger than the circumstances and that He is ultimately in charge. In fact memorize these words (they could save your life):

And have you forgotten the exhortation which addresses you as sons?—"My son, do not regard lightly the discipline of the Lord, nor lose courage [lose faith] when you are punished by Him. For the Lord disciplines him whom He loves, and chastises every son whom He receives." It is for discipline that you have to endure. God is treating you as sons; for what son is there whom his father does not discipline? If you are left without discipline, in which all have participated, then you are illegitimate children and not sons. Besides this, we have had earthly fathers to discipline us and we respected them. Shall we not much more be subject to the Father of spirits and live? For they disciplined us for a short time at their pleasure, but he disciplines us for our good, that we may share his holiness. For the moment all discipline seems painful rather than pleasant; later it yields the peaceful fruit of righteousness to those who have been trained by it.

Therefore lift your drooping hands and strengthen your weak knees, and make straight paths for your feet, so that what is lame may not be put out of joint but rather be healed. Strive for peace with all men, and for the holiness without which no one will see the Lord. See to it that no one fail to obtain the grace of God; that no "root of bitterness" spring up and cause trouble, and by it the many become defiled.

Hebrews 12:5–15

Jesus calls us, His followers, disciples. Here we are told that we are trained by the discipline of painful and trying times. When they come, we must recognize God's presence with us and that He desires to train us through them.

A five-year-old in our church was riding home on the school bus and said to the other boy in his seat, "You better not do that! Your dad might give you a spanking." The other boy answered, "Aw, my dad doesn't spank me." The Christian kid responded, "What's the matter, doesn't he love you?"

Brothers and sisters, God loves us, and He shows us His love by His discipline. No, He doesn't cause the bad times, but He uses the bad times for our good. So we are told, "Count it all joy, my brethren, when you meet various trials, for you know that the testing of your faith produces steadfastness" (James 1:2, 3). We can praise Him, knowing that *all things* work together for good to those who love Him.

Think

1. What caused your hurt the last time you cried?
2. Is it easy or hard for you to pray when you hurt bad? Why?
3. To which authority is it the hardest for you to submit?
4. Why is authority so important? What purpose does it serve?
5. In facing hardships, have you ever felt cheated by God? Describe what it was like.

Act

Memorize Hebrews 12:5–15 (word perfect). It will come in handy for the rest of your life, especially when the roses wilt.

Read

1. You will enjoy reading a whole book on Michelle: Carolyn E. Phillips, *Michelle* (Ventura, Calif.: Regal, 1980).
2. If you have faced a tragedy, you will be helped by reading Philip Yancey, *Where Is God When It Hurts* (Grand Rapids, Mich.: Zondervan, 1977) and another book I wrote, *Growing Pains* (Old Tappan, N.J.: Fleming H. Revell, 1981).
3. Another magnificent book showing one person's response to the hard times is Joni Eareckson and Joe Musser, *Joni* (Grand Rapids, Mich.: Zondervan, 1976); also read Joni Eareckson and Steve Estes, *A Step Further* (Grand Rapids, Mich.: Zondervan, 1979).

10
Yes

An athlete is not crowned unless he
competes according to the rules.
2 Timothy 2:5

Seven years ago a long-haired, confused kid named Wes came to see me. I talked with him only briefly; we prayed together; and as he was walking away I said to myself, *Well, I will never see him again.*

That next year I heard he had gone to Bible college, but I figured he'd never make it. Last summer—six years later—I heard a voice from behind me, "Hey, Fred." I turned, "Do you remember me?" It was Wes. "I just wanted to thank you for going into the ministry and for giving me that advice. Do you remember what you told me?" I was embarrassed, but there was no way I could remember. "You gave me the best advice I ever got. It was simple and just what I needed. You told me, 'Whenever God speaks to you, all you have to do is say Yes.' [I still didn't remember!] I never forgot that advice because *yes* rhymes with my name: *Wes!* That is one policy I have always tried to follow."

Right now he is in the ministry, and yesterday for the first time I heard him preach. He spoke on obedience, and as he stood there before the people, he illustrated his topic by his life of following Jesus.

Being Christians means our lives are governed by two words: *yes* and *no.* The one we say to God, and the other we say to sin.

Following the Rules

Every game has rules that must be followed, or else the contestants will be disqualified. In the 1980 Boston Marathon the famous winner was Rosie Ruiz, who set a women's record of 2:31:56. Claiming, "I ran the race, I really did," she was stripped of her title because she was accused of jumping out of the crowd and running only the end of the race. At the New York Marathon, in which she had finished twenty-third among 1,800 women, officials disqualified her because, in checking their films, they did not see her, and two witnesses even claimed they had seen her in the subways in her running clothes. She ran, but apparently not according to the rules, so she failed to get the prize. As the Bible says, "An athlete is not crowned unless he competes according to the rules" (2 Timothy 2:5).

Elsewhere, Paul put it this way: "Do you not know that in a race all the runners compete, but only one receives the prize? So run that you may obtain it" (1 Corinthians 9:24). This verse used to bother me because to me running meant competition, and I knew Christians should not compete. However the point here is not competition, but dedication and obedience. A runner must be willing to say yes to the rules.

There is nothing in all the world as challenging or as thrilling as getting an assignment from God, saying yes, and then obeying. The only way to live the Christian life is to live by the rules. Jesus even said there is no other way: "If you love me, you will keep my commandments" (John 14:15). If our love for Jesus is genuine, our obedience to Him will follow.

As a young Christian I was driving down the road and a question popped into my head, "Do you love Me?" "Yes, Lord, I love You." "Then why are you speeding?" the Voice asked. I looked at my speedometer and immediately lifted my foot off the accelerator. When my speed matched the speed limit, I let out a shout, "I love You, Jesus!" It made my day to see the relationship between obedience and love for God. This was a small step of obedience, but I tasted what Charles Finney meant by saying, "Revival begins with new obedience to God."

Partial Obedience Is Disobedience

Rosie Ruiz ran part of the race, even the last part, but since she didn't run the whole marathon, she lost.

You can drive the speed limit regularly, but if you speed past the radar gun, the rest of your obedience doesn't matter, and you get a ticket.

We have such a sloppy view of obedience; we think we are doing good when we simply make an effort:

Cutting back from three packs of cigarettes to one.
Only slipping out a few curse words.
Replacing deliberate lying with modest exaggeration.
Giving up fornication for masturbation.

Replacing one sin with another is not what Jesus has in mind. We need to recognize the seriousness of sin.

When I was a senior in high school, my parents got me a nice, dark green Mercury Montego. All Saturday afternoon I spent washing and waxing it for a date I had that night. As I got into the car it just glistened. On my way out the drive, a large crow flew over and dropped a few bombs that hit my hood and windshield broadside. I stopped the car and shook my head, wishing I had my shotgun. *Of all times to get dumped on!* The white crow manure wouldn't have looked so bad if the rest of the car didn't glisten so much.

If we could recognize how foul and perverted sin is, we wouldn't tolerate so much of it.

It makes me sad to be asked, "Can I get an abortion and still be a Christian?" or, "Can I smoke pot, go all the way, commit suicide, and still get to heaven?"

Christians don't ask those questions! No Christian says, "How much can I get away with and still be a Christian?"

A Christian says, "What can I do to be as much like Christ as possible?" Complete obedience is genuine obedience.

Do It Now

When God speaks, He expects action—not *maybe,* not *later,* not *I'll think about it,* but *yes* and *now.* The greatest cop-out from doing what we are supposed to do is procrastination. We usually don't say an emphatic, "No." It's usually, "How about tomorrow? See, I'm really busy and. . . ." The problem is, we are not talking about the request of a friend, a neighbor, a classmate, a boss, a coach, or even a parent; we are talking about Almighty God.

During my freshman year of high school, I lettered in football in the fall and track in the winter. It was now spring, and I had to decide between baseball, track, or tennis. I had played a lot of baseball. It was probably my best sport. I had been on all-county teams and pitched our opening all-star game. However, I decided against playing for my high-school team, since I figured it was time to try something new. I had just finished winter track and was sort of burned out from running around in circles, so I decided to go out for tennis.

I hadn't played much tennis and consequently had never played against anyone a whole lot better than myself. Besides, I figured I could always go out for baseball if I didn't make it at tennis.

The first day of spring practice was very cold. In fact, as I recall, there were snow flurries. I was shaking so badly I could hardly swing the racket. (Good excuse!) All my strokes were short and jerky. I looked more as if I was playing Ping-Pong than tennis. I was getting so few shots in the court that no one even wanted to volley with me.

The next day as I went to the locker room to dress for tennis practice, everyone was gathered around a sheet of paper on the wall. At the top it said, "The Tennis Team," and below were listed the players who made the first cut. My name was not on the list. I couldn't believe it; for the first time in my life, I was cut from the roster. I exchanged my sneakers and racket for my cleats and glove and headed for the baseball diamond. I can still remember what the coach said as I walked onto the field, "Fred, it's too late to try out for the baseball team. You're not in grammar school anymore. This is high school, and you're responsible for your decisions."

Jesus says, ". . . Behold, now is the acceptable time; behold, *now* is the day of salvation" (2 Corinthians 6:2, *italics mine*). We can plan on making things right with God sometime in the future, but someday it will be too late. He says, "Today . . . now." When He gives us an assignment, we need to say, "Yes, Lord, right away."

Our Example

We live in an age of easy diets, instant physical fitness, and miracle cures, so we expect easy answers and instant solutions. Unfortunately it doesn't work that way.

Much like us, the church of Corinth hoped for easy Christianity. Being a sports fan, Paul popped their bubble by referring to both track and boxing:

Do you not know that in a race all the runners compete, but only one receives the prize? So run that you may obtain it. Every athlete exercises self-control in all things. They do it to receive a perishable wreath, but we an imperishable. Well, I do not run aimlessly, I do not box as one beating the air; but I pommel my body and subdue it, lest after preaching to others I myself should be disqualified.

1 Corinthians 9:24–27

When speaking about track, the apostle was referring not to the Boston Marathon, but to the Isthmian Games, which were started by Alexander the Great and held every third year in Corinth, Greece. If you flew to Corinth today, you could see some of the starting blocks still embedded in the stone streets. In order to compete in these Olympic Games, the athletes had to take an oath saying they had trained for at least ten months. It was not just a casual, easygoing affair. It was serious business. Paul made it clear that the Christian life is serious business. It takes training and self-control to gut it out.

Those athletes had to follow the rules. Imagine watching the Olympic Games and suddenly, out of the pack of runners, one heads for the bleachers and begins running through the stands, hopping over people, knocking over vendors and little children. Aimlessly is no way to win a race, and it is no way to live the Christian life. It takes focusing on the goal and at times agonizing over it. Our goal is to be like Jesus, and we need to give ourselves, without reserve, to meet that goal.

The other picture is that of boxing. How hilarious to picture a man stepping into the ring against a champion boxer and frantically beginning to swing at the air. He would work up a real lather and wear himself out, but he would be totally ineffective. His opponent could easily walk over and deck him with a few solid punches.

Most boxing fans agree that Sugar Ray Leonard is one of the finest fighters to step into the ring. But on September 16, 1981, when he was getting beaten into the ropes by the thundering fists of Thomas Hearns, most of the cheering mobs thought he had met his match. All three judges had Hearns ahead when the fight came to an end at 1:45 of the fourteenth round. Fortunately for Sugar Ray, he scored a technical knockout, and the sellout crowd at Caesar's Palace went bananas.

Leonard later admitted, "I was afraid of him right until the very end, and that right is something else. He dropped some real bombs on me."

Why did he win? Guts! In his own words, "I pulled this one out by reaching down into my guts, into my heart. I knew I had to reach down and pull out the reserve and did it . . . I'm sure I surprised a lot of people by putting Hearns down."

Paul described himself as a Christian boxer. (The word used here for "box" is very intense, meaning "to mutilate.") He says he is willing to "pommel" his body. Literally, the Greek word means "to make black and blue." Paul says, "I take my holiness so seriously that I will go to any extent, even to the point of making myself black and blue to resist sin and maintain a righteous holy standard in my life." In no way was he practicing masochism (as if he enjoyed physical injury). Because of such love for Jesus, Paul wanted to be all that God wanted him to be.

Just consider what Paul suffered for being a Christian:

On five different occasions he was whipped thirty-nine times with the cat-o'-nine-tails.

Three times he was beaten with rods.

Once he lived through the popular mode of capital punishment—stoning.

Frequently he was hunted like an outlaw or some wild animal.

Often he gave up food, sleep, and was stripped of all the luxuries of life.

You better believe Paul put his muscle where his mouth was! He stands as a model for us of one person who did it right, who gave it all, 100 percent, to say yes to Jesus always.

There are times to sweat blood, cut off hands, get black eyes, lose sleep, and forego eating meals in order to follow Jesus. After all, He did. And if He lives in us, we can, too.

Not Just Service, but Servants

There is no such thing as a part-time Christian. (If there were, where would he go if he died on the off time?) There is no such thing as a part-time servant. Either you are a full-time servant, or you are no servant at all.

You see, there is a difference between serving the Lord and being a servant of the Lord. Serving is something you do—a verb. A servant is someone you *are*—a noun. Service is something you can accept or reject, but being a servant means, when He speaks, we are ready to obey. Service is part-time. Servant is full-time—100 percent.

Obligation

Sometimes when we do what Jesus asks, we feel as if we are doing Him some big favor. That's why we are such lousy servants. What we need to see is our obligation.

Paul called himself a debtor, and that sense of debt motivated him to give himself 100 percent (Romans 1:14). Knowing he was already forgiven, he was a debtor to the grace of Jesus. As he said, "For the love of Christ controls us ..." or as the Phillips translation says, "The very spring of our actions is the love of Christ" (2 Corinthians 5:14).

Every Christian should nail these words of Jesus to his forehead:

When a servant comes in from plowing or taking care of sheep, he doesn't just sit down and eat, but first prepares his master's meal and serves him his supper before he eats his own. And he is not even thanked, for he is merely doing what he is supposed to do. Just so, if you merely obey me, you should not consider yourselves worthy of praise. For you have simply done your duty!

Luke 17:7–10 TLB

Standing Alone

It's hard to stand alone. It's hard to give your first piano recital, catch a pass in the end zone, or talk in front of an audience. When all eyes are focused on you, with expectation, the self-consciousness is enough to kill.

My first organized sport was baseball. The first year I played first base, and when every ball was pitched, I prayed that it would be hit out of the infield, so I couldn't have anything to do with it. (Maybe that's why we didn't even win a game that year.) The possibility of a ball being hit to me made my skin curl. Being part of the team was fine, but when it became necessary for me to stand alone, forget it!

Standing out in a crowd makes us feel awkward. *What if I drop out? chicken out? flunk out?*

We don't like to stand alone, but as Christians we must. When God speaks, He speaks to each of us alone. *Yes* is a word we say all by ourselves. Before God lets us sing in His choir, He makes us sing a solo.

Just One

One is significant:

Aaron Burr would have become president if he had received one more vote.

Alexander Solzhenitsyn was a single man who stood against the whole Soviet Union, with just a pen.

A single vote made Texas a state.

Three hundred forty-six people were killed in France in one of the worst plane crashes of all history because a single cargo door was not completely shut.

One more vote would have impeached Andrew Johnson.

A lake is made out of millions of single drops of water.

Every person whom God calls, He calls as an individual. That single person is then faced with a decision: *Am I willing to stand alone? Should I break loose from the crowd and its acceptable style and risk rejection by following Jesus?* Almost everytime God asks us to respond, we face that same decision. We need to quit saying, "Why me, Lord?" or "Why not her?" and simply answer, "Yes, if You say so, Lord."

Alone Before the Throne

Accountability can be defined as "the ability to be counted." It is saying to Jesus, "You can count on me."

Our society is getting into the bad habit of blaming bad behavior on just about anything other than the person responsible: a broken home, financial problems, emotional instability, or "the environment." We are so prone to make up excuses that we enjoy having other rationalizations for our problems.

The whole country was shocked when John Hinckley, Jr., was declared "not guilty by reason of insanity," when every person in the United States saw him do it dozens of times on instant replay. What our court system said was, "It's okay, John. You weren't responsible for your own actions." No wonder after the hearing Hinckley admitted that his only regret was he didn't wait a split second longer, so that he could have landed a direct hit on our president. No remorse, no contrition, no repentance, and no move toward adjusted behavior. At first I was angry at John Hinckley, but then I realized that he was only believing what our society had told him.

The human courtroom will never hold us perfectly accountable for our actions, but God does. He wants us to understand that someday we will stand before His throne, all alone, to give account of every deed and every idle word. There will be:

No friends to hide behind
No parents to hold your hands
No crowds to share the blame
No defense attorney to plead your case—except Jesus, if you know
  Him

Life is best lived knowing that someday *I* will stand all alone before His throne. When you look at it that way, it's much easier to say to Him today, "Yes, Jesus, You can count on me."

Think

1. When God asks us to do something, why do we sometimes feel like saying no?
2. Which *rule* of God's do you have problems keeping?
3. "Partial obedience is disobedience." What does this mean? Are there any areas of your life in which you are partially obedient?
4. Imagine dying and standing before Jesus. What current area in your life would be an embarrassment?
5. Explain *obligation*.
6. What did Paul mean when he said, "I pommel my body and subdue it"? Is there any area of your life over which you need to exert such self-control? (If you can't think of any, ask your mom or dad or a close friend.)

Act

Memorize the words of Jesus in John 15:1–11 (word perfect). They will help you say yes a lot more easily the next time He speaks to you.

Read

1. Winkie Pratney, *Doorways to Discipleship* (Minneapolis, Minn.: Bethany House, 1977) is a right-on, refreshing book dealing with godly disciplines and obedience to God.
2. Two dramatic books on men who said yes to God: Richard D. Harvey, *Seventy Years of Miracles* (Alberta, Canada: Horizon House, 1977) and Betty Lee Skinner, *Daws: The Story*

of Dawson Trotman, Founder of the Navigators (Grand Rapids, Mich.: Zondervan, 1975) on the founder of the Navigators.

3. A classic that has sold over 10 million copies, considering what it would be like to live life asking the question, "What would Jesus do?" is Charles Sheldon's *In His Steps* (Old Tappan, N.J.: Fleming H. Revell, 1963).

... Live for the rest of the time in the
flesh no longer by human passions but by
the will of God.
1 Peter 4:2

There is no reason to stand like a punching bag, with our arms dangling at our sides, letting sin beat our faces to a pulp. We need to fight back. Besides saying yes to God, we will never make it until we learn to say no to sin.

Some young people tell me, "But I just can't help it! There is nothing I can do; I just have to sin."

I have started asking, "How hard have you tried? Have you sweat blood?" That's what the Bible says: "In your struggle against sin you have not yet resisted to the point of shedding your blood" (Hebrews 12:4).

We often have such a stained-glass-window view of Jesus that we picture Him with huge forearms, able to knock down temptations like tackling dummies. We picture Him as being so superhuman that His times of testing and temptation became like playacting, with no real struggle.

On the contrary, Jesus is the ". . . one who in every respect has been tempted as we are . . ." (Hebrews 4:15). He fought so hard he ". . . offered up prayers and supplications, with loud cries and tears . . ." (Hebrews 5:7). We read a lot about the blood Jesus shed on the cross and about the blood He shed when He had His back ripped open by the whip, but even before His physical abuse, He suffered great soul anguish during which He sweat bullets of blood (Luke 22:44). Like a great marathon runner, He fought off the temptation to buckle under and quit. Everything—His weary body, His close friends, the religious leaders, and the middle-class masses together—were saying, "Quit! Don't take Yourself so seriously. Just relax." But Jesus wasn't listening to anything except the voice of His Father, saying, "Go for it!" Jesus fought, and He won. He conquered sin; and we can, too. Unfortunately we don't try very hard. We baby ourselves and stand there like punching bags, letting sin pound on us.

Punching Bags

Most sin would stop if we would simply avoid certain situations.

Caroline came to me several times with tears of repentance because her boyfriend kept pestering her to have sex, and she kept giving in. Despite much advice, she kept getting *alone* with him in her house when her parents were gone, in the car late at night, or on the beach.

Max always apologized for his late-night drunken fights, telling me it was his friends who brought the liquor, and once he took the first swig, he couldn't stop. But he still spends most of his time with those same guys.

God asks, "Can a man carry fire to his bosom and his clothes not be burned? Or can one walk upon hot coals and his feet not be scorched?" (Proverbs 6:27, 28).

Jesus put it this way:

And if your hand causes you to sin, cut it off; it is better for you to enter life maimed than with two hands to go to hell, to the unquenchable fire. And if your foot causes you to sin, cut it off; it is better for you to enter life lame than with two feet to be thrown into hell. And if your eye causes you to sin, pluck it out; it is better for you to enter the kingdom of God with one eye than with two eyes to be thrown into hell, where their worm does not die, and the fire is not quenched.

Mark 9:43–48

Those words are so radical some people don't pay any attention to them.

Jesus is saying, "You think your eyesight is so important. Well, your moral purity is worth more than that. You think it's so great to be able to run and jump. Well, it is more important to be holy than to have the use of both feet. You really enjoy using your hands. Personal piety is of greater value than everything you can do with your hands."

This means that there are times when Jesus expects us to avoid even good things that might be acceptable to others, but which would cause us to fall in the mud. It also means that, when we avoid these things, we will be considered by others around us as oddballs—as deformed, maimed, crippled, handicapped fanatics. Jesus is still waiting for His people to look a little unusual.

If ever a generation of Christians had an opportunity to stand out as being radically different from their pagan culture, it is now. The world will count us as strange. In fact, if the world doesn't count us strange, there is something wrong with us as Christians.

Stirring Up the Bee Hive

Sometimes we don't know what a hold sin has over us until we try to resist it.

Hank has smoked grass for eleven years. It was almost as natural as breathing. When we knelt together, he asked Jesus into his life. When we stood, he was filled with excitement because he had been forgiven and filled with a new life.

The next day, when I called Hank to see how he was doing, he said, "Fred, I felt lousy all day. I don't know what has happened. I'm guilty all the time, and I have never felt that way before. Last night I knew I was forgiven, but now I feel condemned every time I smoke a reefer."

I had him get his Bible and turn to Romans 7:7, 8:

... If it had not been for the law, I should not have known sin. I should not have known what it is to covet if the law had not said, "You shall not covet." But sin, finding opportunity in the commandment, wrought in me all kinds of coveteousness. Apart from the law sin lies dead.

"You mean I'm not alone?" Hank chuckled.

When the Holy Spirit comes into an individual, He brings a new standard of living and writes those laws on our hearts. For the first time we experience the power of sin fighting back, because for the first time the power of holiness is also working within us. The standards—laws—of God become like a stick that stirs up the bees of sin which had been peacefully nesting in our hearts. Sin swarms with anger and intensity when its hive is first disturbed. Sin is stubborn and doesn't want to leave.

Temptations in Chains

When it comes to fighting temptation, we need to remember: We are not fighting *for* the victory; we are fighting *from* the victory. In this respect every temptation has a chain on it. It might come screaming out at you and try to sink its teeth into you, but you can step aside and avoid getting hurt.

I jog. A few weeks ago I was out running down the street, thinking about what God meant when He said, "No temptation has overtaken you that is not common to man. God is faithful, and he will not let you be tempted beyond your strength, but with the temptation will also provide the way of escape, that you may be able to endure it" (1 Corinthians 10:13).

All of a sudden a mature German Shepherd jumped out from behind a bush and sprinted right toward me. I didn't even have time to pray. But just as his mouth was fully extended, with jaws opened, ready to enjoy my tasty thigh for dinner, the chain I hadn't noticed became fully extended and jerked his head so fast it nearly broke his neck.

It all happened so fast, I hardly broke my stride, and other than a huge surge of instant adrenaline and few sledgehammer thuds from my heart, I was fine. I even smiled and thought, *No* dog *has overtaken you. . . . God is faithful, and . . . will also provide the way of escape. . . .*

We all face our own peculiar areas of temptation and weakness. Sin lives in every heart. The devil knows just what our weaknesses are and how to attack us when we aren't looking. But here's an important principle that we all need to learn: *We don't have to sin.* God always provides a way of escape, even though at the moment we might be fully convinced we are done for. God has put a chain on every temptation, and as long as we keep our distance, we will be fine.

Forgiving Myself

Believing that God can forgive me is often easier than forgiving myself. But until I am able to forgive myself, God's love hasn't sunk in deep enough.

Every time the question of eternal security came up, Kevin broke out in hives. He had to be convinced over and over again that he was not going to hell. I noticed a pattern: Every time I preached on holiness, I got a phone call from him, in a state of panic, "Fred, I'm sorry to bother you, but when you were preaching it was as if you were talking right to me, and I felt all guilty, as if I weren't good enough to be saved. Am I going to heaven or not?"

If he weren't so sincere, I would have laughed out loud, because his phone calls were so predictable.

One afternoon when the phone rang, knowing it was Kevin, I quickly asked the Father for insight into his need. "Kevin, I don't want to know specifically what it is, but is there *one sin* that sticks out in your mind, which keeps making you feel guilty—one thing you have done that you don't think Jesus could forgive?"

After silence he admitted there was. "How did you know?" he asked.

Over the next twenty minutes Kevin learned a truth that changed his life. He was delivered from his gripping guilt, like a prisoner set free from his cell.

I had him pull out a piece of paper and a pen and draw the following diagram, which was inspired by Bill Gothard. In counterclockwise motion he wrote each step.

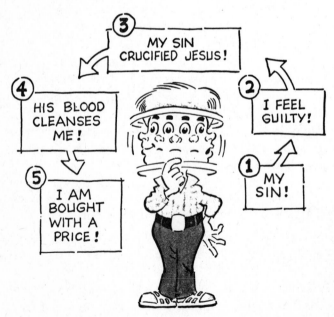

1. "My sin."
2. "I feel guilty."
3. "My sin crucified Jesus."
4. "His blood cleanses me."
5. "I am bought with a price."

1. *"My sin!"*
   That specific sin frequently pops into your brain.
   Agree with God, "You're right! I have sinned by doing_____(name the sin).

   "If we confess our sins, he is faithful and just, and will forgive our sins and cleanse us from all unrighteousness" (1 John 1:9).

2. *"I feel guilty, condemned."*
   As a filthy wretch, you feel unworthy of heaven.
   Again, agree with God: "I am guilty and worthy of eternal judgment."

   "For the wages of sin is death . . ." (Romans 6:23).
   ". . . The soul that sinneth, it shall die" (Ezekiel 18:4 KJV).

3. *"My sin crucified Jesus."*
   Rather than quitting in guilt (step 2), we need to deliberately look to Jesus.
   Visualize yourself nailing Jesus to the cross; driving the stakes through His wrists, thrusting the spear into His side.

   "Surely he has borne our griefs and carried our sorrows. . . . he was wounded for our transgressions, he was bruised for our iniquities . . ." (Isaiah 53:4, 5).

4. *"His blood cleanses me."*
   Jesus not only died because our sins were laid on Him, but His death then removed our sins from us.
   "Thank You, Jesus, for Your cleansing blood. You have done for me what I could have never done for myself; You have relieved me of my guilt and taken away my sin. Praise You!"

   ". . . The blood of Jesus . . . cleanses us from all sin" (1 John 1:7).
   "There is therefore now no condemnation for those who are in Christ Jesus" (Romans 8:1).
   ". . . What God has cleansed, you must not call common" (Acts 10:15).

5. *"I am bought with a price."*

Since you are now forgiven, free from the bondage of sin, you are no longer your own.

"You bought me, Jesus. I want to live for You and use my energies to serve You. Teach me how."

"Do you not know that your body is a temple of the Holy Spirit within you, which you have from God? You are not your own; you were bought with a price. So glorify God in your body" (1 Corinthians 6:19, 20).

". . . live for the rest of the time in the flesh no longer by human passions but by the will of God" (1 Peter 4:2).

"I have been crucified with Christ; it is no longer I who live, but Christ who lives in me; and the life I now live in the flesh I live by faith in the Son of God, who loved me and gave himself for me" (Galatians 2:20).

When I got to the fourth step, Kevin let out a hoot! "Wow! That's just what I needed to hear."

"Now I want you to memorize the diagram," I told him, "and force your mind to go through each step every time that same ugly sin comes across your mind. Then the devil will stop reminding you of it, because it will have a positive effect, rather than a negative."

Kevin has never asked me another question about his eternal life. He knows that he is going to heaven because the love of Jesus has finally enabled him to forgive himself.

Ears to Hear

Jesus expects obedience from His followers: "Blessed are those who hear the Word of God and keep it!" (Luke 11:28).

Unless His followers show obedience, He doesn't want them thinking they are really followers: "Why do you call me Lord, Lord, and not do what I tell you?" A disobedient disciple is no disciple.

As far as Jesus was concerned, it all depended on what kind of ears you have: "He who has ears to hear, let him hear," as He frequently said (Matthew 11:15; *see* also Revelation 2:7, 11, 17, 29; 3:6, 13, 22).

This phrase that was so popular with Jesus used to confuse me until last week, when I was calling my three-year-old daughter for dinner. I stepped outside and said to her as she was getting on her Big Wheel,

"Andrea, it's time for dinner. Come inside and wash up." For a second she looked me right in the eye, then turned and rode her Big Wheel right down our front walk, toward the street. She stopped and turned to look at me, and I firmly restated my case: "Andrea!" She was looking right at me: "I said, it is time to eat dinner. Now come inside immediately!" She proceeded to pedal down the street, turned around in our neighbor's driveway, and looked right at me as if to say, "Okay, let's see, what are you going to do about it?" At this point everyone in the neighborhood could hear me.

The problem was not with her ears. She has two lovely ears, and they were both working fine. The problem was with her *will.*

You have probably seen the comical ads of E. F. Hutton, the investing firm: A busy crowd overhears someone say, "My broker is E. F. Hutton, and he says . . . ," and suddenly everyone freezes. People want financial guidance in these unstable times, because they worship the god of mammon.

Jesus says that genuine Christians will quickly respond to the voice of God. "My sheep hear my voice, and I know them, and they follow me" (John 10:27). Every believer should take that Voice so seriously that he stops dead when he hears, "My God is Jesus Christ, and He says. . . ."

In CB talk, Jesus is saying, "Hey, you got your ears on? C'mon." Are you tuned in to the heavenly channel?

Yes to God and no to sin are a couple of gigantic principles, like inhaling and exhaling oxygen. As Christians, we can't live any other way.

Think

1. Have you felt the power of *sin?* Describe it.
2. Why did Jesus "sweat blood" in the Garden of Gethsemane before He was nailed to the cross?
3. What did Jesus mean when He said, "Cut off your hand ... pluck out your eye?" How can you apply this to your life?
4. Are there certain sins that are impossible to overcome?
5. Name the most active area of temptation in your life.

Act

1. Grab your Bible and read Romans 7. Can you identify? Locate one single sin currently in your life to which you are still in bondage. Then read Romans 6 and break loose.
2. Memorize 1 John 1:9 (I'm being too easy on you—only one verse!)
3. Have you had problems forgiving yourself for any sin from the past? Memorize the five-step diagram in this chapter.

12
Power Plus

And do not get drunk with wine, for
that is debauchery; but be filled with
the Spirit.
Ephesians 5:18

There comes a point in every Christian's life when he discovers that following Jesus is not difficult; it's impossible! (Perhaps several times as you have read through this book you sighed, "This is too much; there's just no way!") Yes, it's true: Living the life God expects of us is a human impossibility. If it were left up to us, we would all fail. Fortunately Jesus didn't leave us hanging by our thumbs.

The Holy Person

When I first met Jesus, I heard the term *Holy Ghost* and I thought of the cartoon character Casper, the Friendly Ghost. When I later heard the term *Holy Spirit,* I pictured the gigantic computer in the Wizard of Oz, which rumbled and billowed smoke. I have since learned the Holy Spirit is not a ghost or a machine or some sort of electric impulse. The Holy Spirit is a Person, and as a Person He experiences many of the things we do.

He has feelings:
 Affection (Romans 15:30)
 Sadness (Ephesians 4:30)
 Rejection (Hebrews 10:29)
He has a will:
 Gives gifts (1 Corinthians 12:11)
 Speaks (Acts 13:2)
 Rebukes, corrects, guides (Acts 16:6, 7)
 Commands (Acts 8:29)
 Leads (Romans 8:14)
He has thoughts:
 Teaches (John 14:26)
 Witnesses (Romans 8:27)

Prays (Romans 8:26)
Searches (1 Corinthians 2:10, 11)
He has desires:
Calls the men He wants (Acts 13:2)
Convicts and convinces (John 16:8–11)

Besides, He is called by the personal pronoun *He,* rather than *it* (John 14:16, 17; 16:7–15).

Not only is the Holy Spirit a Person, but He is a Person who lives right inside every Christian: ". . . Any one who does not have the Spirit of Christ does not belong to him" (Romans 8:9). Now, obviously, if a Christian cuts himself, he will not bleed Jesus, or Jesus will not show up on the screen when a Christian gets X-rayed, but He lives inside us by His Spirit, once we receive Him.

The Indwelling Person

The Holy Person is a mighty One who lives right inside us to provide us with the supernatural strength we need to live the Christian life.

For God is at work in you, both to will and to work for his good pleasure.

Philippians 2:13

. . . He who began a good work in you will bring it to completion at the day of Jesus Christ.

Philippians 1:6

I am the vine, you are the branches. He who abides in me, and I in him, he it is that bears much fruit, for apart from me you can do nothing.

John 15:5

Everytime we say, "Aw, Jesus, I just can't possibly make it," we need to tap our resource—the indwelling Person. Who could do a better job re-creating us than the Creator?

The Abused Person

How do you feel when people:

Interrupt you while you're talking?
Deliberately do what you have asked them not to do?
Make fun of your mother or sister (or someone else you love)?
Treat you as if you don't even exist?

If you are normal, you get a little upset at such abuse. Often, unfortunately, this is exactly how we treat the Holy Person.

There are many ways in which we abuse Him:

Spit in His face by rejecting Him (Mark 3:28–30)
Lie to His face by faking it (Acts 5:3)
Resist by not following His advice (Acts 7:51)
Insult Him and make Him furious (Hebrews 10:29)
Make Him sad by doing things He's told us not to do (Ephesians 4:30)
Throw water on His fire by failing to do what He wants us to do (1 Thessalonians 5:19)

Last night I got up in the middle of the night and stepped right on our cat. The poor little kitty thought it was all over: She ran around in circles and up the walls until the pain subsided. Similarly we will continue to step on and abuse the Holy Person as long as we are in the dark. Knowing that He is always present, with feelings, thoughts, desires, and a will for me should shed some light. Then when I consider the fact that He is Almighty God, I ought to step aside and give Him complete control.

Giving Him Control

Ultimately there is *one way* to treat the Holy Spirit properly: to let Him completely take over my life. Once the Holy Spirit moves in, I need to allow Him to do whatever He wants. Anything less will make both of us miserable and will certainly treat Him as less than God.

In order for Him to take complete control, He needs to completely fill us, and that doesn't happen automatically just because we are Christians. If it did, Paul would have been wasting his time telling the believers in Turkey, "And do not get drunk with wine, for that is debauchery; but be filled with the Spirit" (Ephesians 5:18).

Billy Graham has said, "I believe the greatest need is that men and women who profess the name of Jesus Christ be filled with the Spirit. If you are not filled with the Spirit, you are sinning against God." Right on!

The Explosion in Me

I had been told a lot about *commitment*—giving everything in my life over to Christ's control. For the first five years of my Christian life I was satisfied doing that, but gradually it became like sawdust. Everything I did—reading the Bible, telling others about Christ, teaching Sunday school, showing deeds of kindness, singing hymns and choruses, praying—was all as tasty as sawdust. All the zip was gone. The more I gave myself over to Him, the heavier the burden got.

I started reading anything I could get my hands on that dealt with the Holy Spirit—2,500 pages worth! I interviewed pastors—all kinds—Charismatics, Baptists, Independents. In studying the Word, I came to certain conclusions.

It was wrong to:
  Seek an emotional experience
  Demand any gifts, including tongues
  Get some quick spiritual fix
It was normal for me to:
  Seek all of God
  By faith receive the fullness (or baptism) of the Holy Spirit
  Expect every promise on powerful and victorious living to be mine

There were certain verses I put together:

And do not get drunk with wine, for that is debauchery; but be filled with the Spirit.

Ephesians 5:18

If you then, who are evil, know how to give good gifts to your children, how much more will the heavenly Father give the Holy Spirit to those who ask him!

Luke 11:13

For John baptized with water, but before many days you shall be baptized with the Holy Spirit. . . . But you shall receive power when the Holy Spirit has come upon you; and you shall be my witnesses. . . .

Acts 1:5, 8

Does he who supplies the Spirit to you and works miracles among you do so by works of the law, or by hearing with faith?

Galatians 3:5

And when they had prayed, the place in which they were gathered together was shaken; and they were all filled with the Holy Spirit and spoke the word of God with boldness.

Acts 4:31

If any one thirst, let him come to me and drink. . . . As the Scripture has said, "Out of his heart shall flow rivers of living water."

John 7:37, 38

I will never forget it: February 1, 1975. I got on my knees in our living room, with no one present but the Holy Spirit. I made it clear to God that I was not interested in an emotional experience, nor was I seeking some particular gift. What I was after was the fullness of God—nothing more, nothing less. I prayed through each of the above verses and then said something similar to this:

Jesus, in no way am I ungrateful for my salvation, because Your death for me is the greatest expression of love I will ever know. I was an unworthy wretch when Your grace reached out to me. I know I am saved, but now I have a deep longing in my soul. I need to know I have all of God without measure, and I know that You desire to fill me. So, right now, fill me; saturate me—every area of my life, every cell of my body, every thought. Immerse me in Thy Spirit. I receive this by faith, and I will never again doubt whether or not I have been filled. I know I am filled. Praise You. In Jesus' Name, amen.

I got up off my knees and sat in a chair. There was no lightning bolt that struck me behind the ear, but there was a deep assurance that I had prayed a prayer Jesus wanted me to pray, and I had faith that I had received the fullness of God. I quietly sang to Jesus, and great joy filled my soul.

The next three months were filled with mellow excitement. Seven very distinct changes came into my life. They all happened so fast, it was like trying to hold onto a live wire. In abbreviated form, here are the seven changes:

Deep conviction of sin: The burden got so great, I had to call several people and ask them for forgiveness. I had never noticed before what a cesspool bubbled in my heart!

Praise: Songs and choruses were sung with delight, and even when things went wrong, I was able to rejoice.

Prayer: I couldn't spend enough time on my knees. God gave me a system of prayer cards from which I have seen hundreds of answers (and hundreds of *un-answers!*).

Miracles: God became so real that I asked Him for things I would never have thought to ask Him about before—fix the oven and broken tape player—and miracles happened.

The fruit of the Spirit (Galatians 5:22, 23): Certainly I am far from a finished product, but immediately I began having desires to show deeds of love as never before.

Gifts of the Spirit: Soon after, several spiritual gifts were manifested in my life—things I hadn't even expected.

Power in ministry: Both in personal evangelism at a nearby college and in preaching at a local church, people gave their lives to Christ, whereas I had ministered for years without seeing much response.

This list is not meant to represent everything that happens when you get filled with the Spirit; they are simply the things that happened to me.

There were probably other things, but these were the obvious changes. The Christian life was no longer just me committing and committing and committing. Obviously I was committed, but the ultimate responsibility for my personal holiness shifted from my shoulders to Christ's.

My life is not a bowlful of cherries. I still have trials and temptations and hard times, but I enjoy an overall joy and satisfaction of fellowship with Jesus because I have stepped aside and given the Holy Spirit control.

The Number-One Mark

F. B. Meyer, famous Bible teacher, knew what he was talking about when he identified the primary function of the Holy Spirit: "He is like a shaft of light that falls on the Beloved Face, so that as in the photograph you do not think about the light nor the origin of the light, but you think about the face it reveals." The face he is referring to is that of Jesus.

Jesus agrees: "He [the Holy Spirit] will glorify me . . ." (John 16:14). This means that when our joy over singing, praying, and Bible reading gets old or our love for Jesus gets cold, it's a problem with the way we are treating the Holy Spirit.

You can stand in a gymnasium or out in the middle of a field and not hear a sound. But potentially there are sounds all around us, if only we had an AM or FM receiver to pick up the radio waves. The waves are always there, but without the receiver and tuner, we could flap our arms feverishly or stand on our heads with antennae between our toes and never pick up a single station.

So the Holy Spirit tunes us in to Jesus and in to His Word. When we are filled with the Spirit, His message comes in loud and clear, as if Jesus was right there with us—because, in fact He is!

The number-one mark of being filled with the Holy Spirit is not speaking in tongues: It is an intense love for Jesus. That is, after all, the mark of a Christian, which motivates a radical love for others.

Once Is Not Enough

God cannot use a person who is just a little wet behind the ears; He wants His people drenched! Soaked in the Spirit! There is only one way to be filled: 100 percent!

The filling is not a one-stage rocket that puts us in orbit for the rest of our days. There needs to be an initial crisis that often (but not always) is accompanied by dramatic changes, but there also needs to be a daily, continuous filling. When we are told to "be filled with the Spirit," it means to be filled initially and continuously. A lake that is filled once and never again quickly gets stagnant and eventually dries up. But a lake that is alive and vibrant always has fresh water flowing. That's right where Jesus wants us: hooked up to the constant flow of His Spirit, enjoying the refreshment and vitality of the growing Christian life.

A Case Study

Albert Simpson had been a Christian for a long time. In fact, in 1875 he had been a minister for more than ten years, but he knew there was something missing. His inner hunger led him to seek God and read anything about his hunger pains. Both for his own personal piety and for his effectiveness in reaching out to others, He searched for the power he needed.

As his search reached its climax, here's how he described it:

Throwing myself at the feet of my glorious Master, just at that time God poured out His Spirit upon my own heart. It was then that I received for the first time the new light of the indwelling Christ and the baptism of the Holy Spirit. It became a fire in my bones and so possessed me that nights long I waited before God crying to Him for a great revival.

Soon after this crisis, Simpson organized a citywide evangelistic crusade in Louisville, Kentucky, where he was pastoring, and he saw more souls saved than ever before in his ministry; 5,000 to 6,000 came to Christ! This was the beginning of the great harvest, and it started with the consecrated life of A. B. Simpson. He was used to begin the great missionary enterprise of the Christian and Missionary Alliance, and the fires still brightly shine. Many of Simpson's old associates rejected his friendship because of his openness to the fullness of the Holy Spirit, but that was part of the cost. He wanted power rather than popularity, and God mightily used him.

Simpson wrote about the fullness of the indwelling Christ in the poem "Himself."

Once it was the blessing, now it is the Lord;
Once it was the feeling, now it is His Word.
Once His gifts I wanted, now the Giver own;
Once I sought for healing, now Himself alone.

Once 'twas painful trying, now 'tis perfect trust;
Once a half salvation, now the uttermost.
Once 'twas ceaseless holding, now He holds me fast;
Once 'twas constant drifting, now my anchor's cast.

Once 'twas busy planning, now 'tis trustful prayer;
Once 'twas anxious caring, now He has the care.
Once 'twas what I wanted, now what Jesus says;
Once 'twas constant asking, now 'tis ceaseless praise.

Once it was my working, His it hence shall be;
Once I tried to use Him, now He uses me.
Once the power I wanted, now the Mighty One;
Once for self I labored, now for Him alone.

Once I hoped in Jesus, now I know He's mine;
Once my lamps were dying, now they brightly shine.
Once for death I waited, now His coming hail;
And my hopes are anchored, safe within the vail.

Jesus has already told you, "Be filled with the Spirit." What have you done about it?

Think

1. Since the Holy Spirit is a Person who lives inside every Christian, how do you treat Him? How do you mistreat Him?
2. Describe in your own words what it means to be filled with the Spirit.
3. What is the main purpose of the Holy Spirit in the life of Christians? What are other purposes?
4. In what ways have you observed the Holy Spirit acting in your life?

Act

Can you identify with the deep spiritual hunger I experienced before praying to receive the filling of the Spirit? If so, read through and pray through the verses I have listed in the chapter.

Read

If A. B. Simpson gets your juices flowing, you will enjoy reading both his biographies: A. W. Tozer, *Wingspread* (Harrisburg, Pa.: Christian Publications) and A. E. Thompson, *A. B. Simpson, His Life and Work* (Harrisburg, Pa.: Christian Publications).

13
Kneeling

"But when you pray, go into your room
and shut the door and pray to your Father
who is in secret; and your Father who sees
in secret will reward you."
Matthew 6:6

Prayer is communication between one person and God. As followers of Jesus we need to do everything necessary to keep our channels of communication open; weeds choke the unused path.

Many years ago King George V was ready to speak on international radio from Britain, relayed by cable to America. Just as the broadcast was about to begin, the main electric cable snapped in the New York radio station. The station manager and staff panicked: 1 million listeners were waiting to hear the king's voice in moments, and the cable would take at least twenty minutes to fix. Suddenly a junior mechanic, Harold Vivien, saw what needed to be done. He grabbed both ends of the cable and held them together, allowing the current to communicate the royal message. From head to toe, his body convulsed with pain as 200 to 250 volts of electricity pulsated through him, but he never loosed his grasp.

God is looking for young men and women like Harold Vivien, who will never relax their grasp in prayer, laying hold of the needs of the people with one hand and laying hold of Almighty God with the other. Others can stand off at a distance and pout, but the Lord Jesus is looking for someone to pray.

Prayer Problems

Prayer is easier to talk about than it is to do. It's so easy to say, "Hey, I'll be praying for you," and just as easy to forget. We find it hard to talk to our lab partners or friends in the lunchroom, let alone having to talk with Almighty God! Some of us just don't like to be alone. Others of us find it hard to believe that Jesus really takes us seriously. When we start to pray, we wonder if God has His receiver off the hook. But until we overcome such barriers and establish a set daily prayer time, we will never get anywhere as Christians.

Jesus, the Man of Prayer

As His disciples we have no better model pray-er than the Lord Jesus. Let these verses bounce back and forth in your brain:

The next morning he was up long before daybreak and went out alone into the wilderness to pray.

Mark 1:35 TLB

But word of him spread even more, and large crowds gathered to listen and to be healed of their diseases. Jesus, however, habitually withdrew into the desert for prayer.

See Luke 5:15, 16

He dismissed the crowd, and after he had taken leave of them, went away to the mountain to pray.

See Mark 6:46

One day soon afterwards he went out into the mountains to pray, and prayed all night. At daybreak he called together his followers and chose twelve of them to be the inner circle of his disciples. . . .

Luke 6:12, 13 TLB

Jesus did not allow His busy schedule to keep Him from prayer. When necessary, He would get up and pray before breakfast or even stay up and pray through the night. Even though He loved being with people, His time with His heavenly Father was more important. If Jesus considered it essential to give Himself to a life of prayer, how much more should we.

Don't think Jesus is unique as a man of prayer. There are many Christians who have followed His devotional life.

Martin Luther said, "If I fail to spend two hours in prayer each morning, the devil gets the rest of the day. I have so much business I cannot get on without spending three hours daily in prayer."

George Verwer, founder of Operation Mobilization (an international missionary enterprise) frequently spends whole nights in prayer.

Scottish preacher John Welch feels as if he has wasted the day if he doesn't spend eight to ten hours on his knees. His wife complained of finding him lying on the ground, crying. He responded to her, "Woman, I have the souls of three thousand to answer for, and I know not how it is with many of them."

John Wesley, who spent two hours daily in prayer, said, "God does nothing but in answer to prayer."

Charles Simeon woke early and prayed from 4:00 to 8:00 A.M. every day.

These guys are not just an isolated band of fanatics. They are followers of Jesus who prayed the way He did.

Here are three helpful tips on how to establish a daily time of prayer.

My Prayer Closet

Genuine prayer will never be popular: You will never see it in flashing neon lights; it will never replace "Monday Night Football." Prayer is not popular, because prayer is private. Until we get that through our skulls, real prayer won't happen.

Just listen to Jesus:

"And when you pray you must not be like the hypocrites; for they love to stand and pray in the synagogues and at the street corners, that they may be seen by men. Truly, I say to you, . . . go into your room and shut the door and pray to your Father who is in secret; and your Father who sees in secret will reward you."

Matthew 6:5, 6

I think you understand *closet* does not mean the place we hang our clothes. It's not to be taken literally. A closet is a private place, where we can go without interruption and distractions, a place where we can quietly keep secrets with God.

To the average teenager, to sit for more than five minutes means you are either in front of a TV or at an athletic event. To close your door, turn off the stereo, and take the phone off the hook to spend moments alone—just you and Jesus—might sound boring. "Yeah, and my faith is about the size of a raisin!" you add. As far as Jesus is concerned, with that much faith, "You can say to this mountain, 'Be cast into the sea,' and it shall be done for you" (*see* Mark 11:23).

You need a starting point. Pick a place—your room, basement, attic, den, treehouse—where you can meet with God daily, without interruption.

My Prayer Time

I love to fish. I am willing to get up at 6:00, 5:00, or even 4:00 A.M. to go. One night several years ago I was out until 2:00 A.M. surf casting for snook—a big game fish in south Florida. I set my alarm and got up at 4:30 (two and a half hours later) to go out in a boat to try some trolling. Without effort, my body hopped up, slipped into my jeans and T-shirt and headed for the bathroom. My thoughts of catching the big one were interrupted by what seemed like the Voice of God, "Why can you get up so enthusiastically to go catch fish, when you can't get up to meet with Me?" That was like getting hit in the head with a tuna fish!

I staggered back and sat on the edge of the bed, hung my head low, and shook it. I got the message: It was a matter of motivation. I was up because I loved to fish, and there is nothing wrong with that. But my failure to get up to meet with Jesus said something gross about my love for Him.

What we want to do, we find time to do. God also showed me that another reason I was up was because I made an appointment to meet my friend. I knew he was expecting me to be ready. Certainly God is available all the time, and we are told to "pray without ceasing" (1 Thessalonians 5:17 KJV) but if we are going to grow and develop the way we should, we need to spend special, uninterrupted private time with Him—just the two of us.

For those special times, it is helpful to make an appointment with Him—to say as you're turning the lights out, "Lord Jesus, I'll see You in the morning. Let's make it 6:15 A.M." Then you are obligated not to get up at 6:15, but to be ready to meet with Jesus at 6:15, which means taking care of bathing, drying, combing, brushing, spraying, dressing, and who knows what else prior to 6:15. Then when you kneel down in the room with just you and Jesus and His Word, say, "Here I am, Lord, 6:15! I told You I'd make it."

Once we pick a place and a time to pray daily, we still need to know how.

My Prayer System

In order to pray consistently and effectively in the closet, we each need our own prayer system. There are many varieties:

A prayer sheet, with a list of names and needs
A prayer journal, almost like a diary of written conversations to God
A prayer notebook, with separate pages for each specific need, with answers recorded under every heading

I have used each of these, but the most effective system is prayer cards, which I have now been using for eight years.

It all started with the verse "Continue steadfastly in prayer, being watchful in it with thanksgiving" (Colossians 4:2). I knew I wasn't steadfast or watchful or thankful. I prayed, but there was no consistency. Then I received a mailing on prayer that greatly impressed me, listing specific answers to prayer:

San Bernadino, California—15 praying
9/73 That the commander at Norton Air Force Base would give up the chapel . . . to us for Sunday School space.
3/74 We have the old chapel! We built it into Sunday School space and over 100 children hear Bible teaching each Sunday.
Alma, Michigan—Many groups praying
8/72 That the parents of 5-year-old Greg would turn to God . . . during his treatment for cancer.
5/73 Greg lived 1½ years after his diagnosis and during that time his parents, grandmother and great aunt all came to know the Lord. Greg told his mother during the quiet hours of one of the sleepless nights that "he didn't know why, he loved her and Daddy and his

sister, but he loved God and Jesus more." He only had a brief experience in church prior to his illness.

Larwill, Indiana—6–10 praying

4/73 Praying for Tony Licata, a 4-year-old boy with a malignant tumor. Doctors had done all they could for him.

12/73 In examining the boy, the doctors discovered there were no longer signs of the tumor. Praise God for this miracle.

I wanted to see such specific answers to my prayers. I took a stack of three-by-five cards, and being sensitive to the Holy Spirit, I wrote out specific burdens in the form of prayer requests, with the date on the top of the card. I started out with only five such cards. By the end of the first week I had one answer. I wrote the date and then how God answered what I had prayed. I was excited! That card was the first in a new pile of answered-prayer cards. Before the end of the first month I had seen six specific answers to prayer, and I had a stack of thirty individual prayer cards that I was praying through each day.

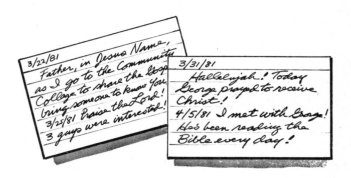

3/22/81 Father, in Jesus Name, as I go to the Community College to share the Gospel, bring someone to know You! 3/25/81 Praise the Lord! 3 guys were interested!

3/31/81 Hallelujah! Today George prayed to receive Christ! 4/5/81 I met with George! He's been reading the Bible every day!

Today I have a large stack of answered-prayer cards. They are all to the glory of God's grace, and they help remind me that prayer works. Now I am able to be steadfast, watchful, with thanksgiving in prayer. Whenever the devil whispers in my ear, "Aw, why pray? God doesn't pay any attention to you," all I have to do is point to my answered-prayer cards and say, "You liar!"

If you have no other effective prayer system, pick up a few three-by-five cards. Start this godly habit; it will help keep your channels of communication open. Just remember, when your faith is the size of a raisin, don't begin with a three-hour prayer time with 500 prayer cards. Like a muscle, let your faith develop by consistent daily exercise.

Prayer Partners

When I was in the tenth grade, one afternoon I was at a friend's house, listening to music. I don't know what got into me, but I walked over, turned off the stereo, and said, "Let's pray." He stared at me as if I had asked him to dance. "Come on, I'm serious; we both know Jesus—let's pray!" We just started talking to Him as if He was our Friend (which He was). Ten or fifteen minutes later, when we finished, we looked at each other and he said, "Wow! Why didn't we ever do that before?"

While real prayer starts in the closet—keeping secrets between me and Jesus, which no one else will ever know about—it sure helps to pray with a friend. You might be the only Christian kid you know in your high school or at your office, but ask God for a prayer partner whom you can meet with once every week. You don't need to pray for a whole hour; even if it's only two minutes, it will be better than nothing.

Jesus had this in mind when He said, "Again I say to you, if two of you agree on earth about anything they ask, it will be done for them by my Father in heaven. For where two or three are gathered in my name, there am I in the midst of them" (Matthew 18:19, 20).

It sure is great to have someone you can call to ask to pray for you when you are down in the dumps, tempted, feeling sorry for yourself, studying for a big exam, or even hoping to get a date for the hayride. Wouldn't it be nice to have someone come up to you and ask, "Will you be my prayer partner?" Well, don't wait for him or her; you ask someone.

Prayer Meetings

Every Christian needs to meet regularly with other Christians for prayer, and every church and every youth group needs a prayer meeting. That's what the early church did, and I would say it was pretty effective:

... They were all gathered together in one place. And suddenly a sound came from heaven like the rush of a mighty wind, and it filled the house where they were sitting. And there appeared to them tongues as of fire, distributed and resting on each one of them. And they were all filled with the Holy Spirit....

Acts 2:1–4

And when they had prayed, the place in which they were gathered together was shaken; and they were all filled with the Holy Spirit and spoke the word of God with boldness.

Acts 4:31

Why don't we see power like that? Because we don't see prayer like that!

I had fun leading a group of teenagers in Hamilton, Massachusetts, who took Jesus seriously. We had met for a seven-week discipleship group. Rather than stopping when the seven weeks were done, they decided to keep meeting regularly for prayer. At the first Saturday morning God inspired us to pray two prayers: that Holy Spirit revival would come to Boston and that it would be reported on the front page of the *Boston Globe* and that God would give us 1,000 Bibles to pass out to every student in the local high school.

A month later I was walking along, and a man came up to me and said, "I understand you want Bibles. I have four hundred, would you like them?" Praise the Lord! When I brought them to our next prayer meeting, there was a lot of shouting and stomping and praising the Lord.

Two weeks went by until our next group prayer meeting. As we met for prayer a girl brought in the morning paper. The headlines read, "Awakening in Boston" (or something to that effect)!

With such encouragement to our faith, we kept meeting for prayer. Several from the high school were meeting Christ, and the Bibles were being distributed faithfully, but we still needed 600 additional Bibles to give one to each student.

I received a letter several months later from the same Bible society that printed the Bibles we had been giving out. The letter read, "We are thrilled you are distributing God's Word in the public high school. Do

you need any more Bibles? We have 600 copies of that printing left."
The original 400 plus this 600 made the 1,000 for which we have been
praying.

Intercessors for America newsletter (January 1976) contained the following exciting account: Christians from Traverse City, Michigan, were
united in prayer, claiming that God was going to stop the "glitter rock
band" KISS from performing, as the band openly calls on demons during
their concerts. The young believers even told their classmates the KISS
concert would not happen. Many Christians were praying behind the
scenes the very moment the concert was to begin. Six thousand young
people (average age sixteen to seventeen years old) showed up at the
Glacier Dome concert hall. Many of them knew Christians were praying
against the concert. *Coincidentally* twelve thousand dollars' worth of the
band's electronic equipment blew up! After an hour of attempted repair
work, the crowd was turned away. No concert in answer to prayer.

When we take God seriously in prayer, He takes our prayers seriously.
If we want to see the power, God needs to see the prayer. If you are interested in starting a prayer meeting, be sure to keep your prayers specific, and be sure to pray for those things that would be impossible apart
from God's miraculous power. Unless you step out in faith and pray for
miracles, you will never see them.

"Thanks"

Thus far we have only dealt with one dimension of prayer—*asking*.
There is another dimension we have missed completely—*thanking*.

We need to thank Jesus for *what He does:*

Thank Him for every part of your body that functions properly.
Thank Him for each member of your family.
Thank Him for your friends.
Thank Him for your possessions.
Thank Him for your country.
Thank Him for your abilities and talents.
Ultimately thank Him for dying on the cross for your sins.

And we need to thank Him for *Who He is.*

Which one of these qualities of God have you experienced personally? In what ways?

Love	Health and Life
Forgiveness	Never changing
Patience	Eternal
Holiness	Truth
Omnipresence	Goodness
Wisdom	Justice
Power	

In praying through my prayer cards every day, I have found it helpful to spend my prayer time, every Friday, just thanking Jesus for the condition of each request. Since I believe Jesus is Lord over every area of life, I can praise Him regardless of how hopeless any given situation might seem.

Probably the most common word in prayer is *please.* When I was in high school, someone who always begged for things was called a moocher. The Lord Jesus is often "mooched off of" by ungrateful children who barge into His presence, bark out their demands, and then stomp out without any exchange of affection or appreciation.

The most common words in prayer should be *thank You.* God likes to hear that we think He's doing a good job. In fact our whole lives are meant to say, "Thanks," to God.

Think

1. What excuses do people use for not praying?
2. What is a *prayer closet?* Why is this a practical idea?
3. Do you spend more time in prayer saying *please* or *thank You?*
4. Why is it so important to be involved in a prayer meeting?

Act

1. Pick a prayer closet where you can meet alone with God every day.
2. Schedule a time slot of fifteen minutes to meet here every day to pray and read the Bible. Make the appointment.
3. Establish some prayer system. (Use three-by-five cards if you have no better system.)
4. If you do not have a prayer partner, begin praying for someone. When someone appropriate comes to mind, ask him or her to consider it and then meet together once a week. (Try not to miss.)

Read

1. A red-hot book on prayer that is a *must:* Edward M. Bounds *Power Through Prayer* (Grand Rapids, Mich.: Zondervan, 1962). It's a zinger!
2. Two biographies on outstanding men of Christianity; Norman Grubb, *Rees Howells; Intercessor* (Fort Washington, Pa.: Christian Literature Crusade, 1952); Arthur T. Pierson, *George Muller of Bristol* (Old Tappan, N.J.: Fleming H. Revell, 1971).

14
Honest to God

And before him no creature is hidden, but
all are open and laid bare to the eyes of
him with whom we have to do.
Hebrews 4:13

When Jesus came to earth and lived in Israel, He loved everyone. He specialized in loving the unlovely: the drunks, the pimps, the prostitutes, the gluttons, and even those involved in organized crime. He was kind to the simple folk and always reached out to help the poor and physically handicapped. But there was one group He just couldn't handle: the *fakers*.

Easy Does It

There are times when we all feel self-conscious, a little insecure inside; we wonder if we are making a good impression. In a crowded bus, cafeteria, or busy locker room, it is easy to:

Act as if everything is cool, when underneath you don't feel cool.
Smile big, when inside you feel small and awkward.
Pretend that everyone is your friend, when really you feel all alone.

It's easy to be a faker. We don't like it when others do it, and we don't like it when we do it, but sometimes when we feel uncool and awkward and lonely, we don't know what else to do.

There are all kinds of fakers.

Athletic Fakers

Peter kept telling me what a great golfer he was. Every time I asked him, I couldn't understand why he never wanted to play. Finally, when his excuses ran out and I got him on the course, I found out why: He talked a better game than he played. The day we played, he could have written a book on excuses for not playing good golf. I felt bad for Peter, because he was a good kid, but I wished he didn't try to impress me so much. If he had been himself, we could have become better friends.

Social Fakers

So often behind nice clothes are feelings of guilt; behind muscular bodies are insecurities; behind a big, pretty smile is loneliness. Well, no one likes to feel guilty, insecure, and lonely, so we fake it.

Moral Fakers

Most kids hide something from their parents because they know it's wrong: dirty magazines, smoking behind the barn, or kissing in the woods after school.

I met a guy at camp who had a whole field of marijuana growing behind his house without his parents knowing anything about it.

I have heard many kids give glowing testimonies at Sunday-evening church, only to shift into overdrive in the backseat of some car after the service with a boyfriend or girl friend.

Playing the Fool

Nobody likes a faker. In fact, a faker doesn't like himself; if he did, he wouldn't need to fake it.

When it comes right down to it, you can't even get to know a faker. Just when you think you know him, you find out he was only wearing a mask. Faking can become a very serious problem when we start fooling ourselves. When we have lived a lie long enough, our perception of reality will get so blurred that lies become truth and truth becomes a dream. That's scary!

The saying is sure: "You may fool all the people some of the time; you can even fool some of the people all the time; but you can't fool all of the people all the time. [And you can't fool God any of the time.]"

Just listen to this: "And before him no creature is hidden, but all are open and laid bare to the eyes of him with whom we have to do." (Hebrews 4:13). Why do we even try to hide from God?

Sweet Honesty

The basis of any relationship is honesty—to be able to say, with your head up and shoulders back, without any apologies, "This is me; take it or leave it." It's true socially, and it's true spiritually. Until we quit hiding things from God, we'll never get anywhere with Him. For some reason, even though we know He knows, we still try to cover up and hide things, thinking we're keeping them to ourselves as if God were not involved.

Hidden Hurts

Pain can drive us deep within ourselves, to where we think we are the only ones who know what it feels like. "What would God know about such suffering and grief?" we question.

I will never forget praying with Glenda the night after she was gang raped by a motorcycle gang. She'd never before heard that Jesus loved her personally, and after several hours of sharing and Bible reading together, she opened her heart to His love and asked Him to come in and forgive her and make her a new person. The tears she cried were big, hard tears. Later when I asked her why she'd been so deeply moved, she said, "No one has ever loved me before. I never thought anyone would understand my pain."

Jesus does understand pain. He is called ". . . a man of sorrows, and acquainted with grief . . ." (Isaiah 53:3 KJV). He is able ". . . to sympathize with our weaknesses . . ." (Hebrews 4:15), and He says to those who hurt, "Come unto me all ye that labor and are heavy laden, and I will give you rest. Take my yoke upon you, and learn of me; for I am meek and lowly in heart; and ye shall find rest unto your souls. For my yoke is easy, and my burden is light" (Matthew 11:28–30 KJV).

It doesn't pay to hide our hurts and hurt alone. When we hurt, Jesus wants us to tell Him about it.

Hidden Weaknesses

It's hard to admit weakness and insecurities to God. *After all,* we wonder, *what does Almighty God know about weakness? He has it all together.*

Paul the apostle was a pretty independent guy. He was successful and famous, with an impressive pedigree as long as your arm. Even when he met Jesus, he became an instant Christian celebrity in the eyes of many.

But God allowed him to develop a weakness; Paul called it "a thorn in the flesh." It was hard for him to handle. Over and over he prayed, but but those prayers that seemed to work powerfully for others didn't do a thing for him. Then the Holy Spirit spoke loud and clear: "My grace is sufficient for you, for my power is made perfect in weakness ..." (2 Corinthians 12:9).

This is a principle we all need to learn: *Weakness kept to ourselves makes us weaker; weakness opened to God becomes strength.* Jesus knows when we feel uncoordinated, stupid, ugly, unlovable. At those times we need to tell Him.

Hidden Sin

Sometimes couples mess around, thinking no one will ever know until the girl is shocked to find herself pregnant. All too often we trick ourselves into thinking God isn't watching, either.

For a long time Bret faked his spirituality. He kept hanging around church and the youth group, even though it was obvious to most he was not really walking with the Lord. Finally, when it appeared in the papers that he was busted with cocaine, his hypocrisy got too much, so he stopped pretending and admitted the Christian life was not for him. Unfortunately, when I talked with him about his relationship with Jesus, he wouldn't answer. He would admit his life-style to people, but not to God. All he said was, "It's too late!"

There is a pattern here: once a bloody dagger is hidden in the closet, it leads to more and more cover up. Little lies snowball into big lies, until whole relationships are ruined. It doesn't pay to keep things from God.

We say, "Aw, just this one little sin. It won't matter." Then we say, "Nobody's perfect; just this one bad habit." Finally, "It's too late."

Jesus says, "You faker!" His Word says, "This people honors me with their lips, but their heart is far from me; in vain do they worship me ..." (Matthew 15:8, 9).

Hidden Areas of Our Lives

It's easy to kneel in superficial sincerity and pray, "O Lord, I dedicate my life completely, one hundred percent, to you. Use me any way you want," and then proceed to take it all back piece by piece.

Dating: "God, You just don't know much about dating, so it will be better if I take care of this one. After all, You know how much I feel for_____."

Reputation: "I trust You, Lord with my soul, but I think I'd better watch out for my reputation. I wouldn't want to turn anyone off. You know, Lord."

Future: "My life is Yours, Lord, and I'll show You just what to do with it."

Possessions: "I'll give You Yours and the rest is mine. Right, Lord?"

Time: "My time is Yours, God—anything You say is fine by me—between 9:00 A.M. to noon Sunday morning."

Hobbies: "I put in time reading the Bible a few minutes this morning. I sure am glad, Lord, You let me do what I want for the rest of the day."

Jesus cries, "Not every one who says to me, 'Lord, Lord' shall enter the kingdom of heaven, but he who does the will of my Father who is in heaven" (Matthew 7:21).

I read a true account of a married couple who sold some real estate and pretended to give the full payment to the Lord through their local church, when in fact they kept back a slice of the pie for themselves. The pastor somehow discerned the deceitful plot and said, "You faker! You have not lied to men, but to God." When the man heard those words, he immediately fell over stone dead.

To cap it all off, when his wife came looking for her husband a few hours later, she, too, lied about the money. The pastor said, "Look, the feet of them who buried your husband are at the door, and they will carry you out." And immediately she dropped dead. (Needless to say, fear spread through the church.)

The word went out, "Wow! You can't keep anything from God!" (You can read this true story for yourself in Acts 5:1–11.) If only we could learn not to keep any area of our lives from the Lord.

To Hell With Fakers

We have already seen the difference between a *faker* and a *failure*.

Faker: Someone who acts like he is a Christian, when he isn't.

Failure: Someone who acts like he isn't a Christian, when he is.

There is a big difference.

Matthew 23 contains some of the sharpest words shot from the mouth of Jesus. He is talking to the religious fakes, and he fires seven woes. Let's look at the sixth:

> "Woe to you, scribes and Pharisees, hypocrites! for you are like whitewashed tombs, which outwardly appear beautiful, but within they are full of dead men's bones and all uncleanness. So you also outwardly appear righteous to men, but within you are full of hypocrisy and iniquity."
>
> Matthew 23:27, 28

They were one thing on the surface and another in their hearts. They had such a shallow view of God, they figured He couldn't see beneath the surface. But He sees it all.

This may shock you, but God has a microfilm library where He stores everything we have ever done, said, and thought. It's all on file. And one day we will have to give account for all careless words and bad attitudes and filthy deeds. He will separate His genuine children from the illegitimate fakes. He says about fakers, "And then will I declare to them, 'I never knew you; depart from me, you evildoers'" (Matthew 7:23).

Honestly, Now

David was a man after God's own heart (*see* Acts 13:22). When he was happy, he'd tell God. When he was hunted, he'd tell God. When he was dry and empty, he'd tell God. In every experience he had, he enjoyed the presence of God. But he did one thing that he thought God would never notice.

He was all alone on his balcony. As he looked across the courtyard he spotted a shapely young lady taking a bath. He brought her clearly into focus, and suddenly there was nothing he wanted more. He sent for her, and he got her. They committed adultery. She got pregnant. He sent her husband to the front lines of battle, where he would get killed. Nine months later, the baby was born, became ill, and died, and finally David broke. He couldn't hold it back any longer. It was time to quit hiding and start confessing. Fortunately his exact words were recorded for us.

There was a time when I wouldn't admit what a sinner I was. But my dishonesty made me miserable and filled my days with frustrations. All day and all night your hand was heavy on me. My strength evaporated like water on a sunny day until I finally admitted all my sins to you and stopped trying to hide them. . . .

Psalms 32:3–5 TLB

We are told to confess: "If we confess our sins, he is faithful and just to forgive us our sins, and to cleanse us from all unrighteousness" (1 John 1:9 KJV). The word *confess* in the Greek is *homologeo,* which means "same wording" or "say the same." When we sin, we are to admit it—to say the same thing God says about it. And when we hurt, feel insecure, get frustrated, feel lonely, or even ready to burst with excitement, God wants you to tell Him about it.

Will you come out from under the covers—no more hiding? Will you live in the light of His love and be honest to God?

Before this book starts collecting dust on the shelf, let's take off the masks, slice off the bologna, and quit pretending. When we get right down to it, there is only one way to live, and that is to live 100 percent for Christ. If we are going to bear the name *Christian,* called after the One who gave Himself 100 percent for us, there is no way we can do any less for Him.

"Jesus, I'm Yours—all Yours, 100 percent!"

Think

1. Do you know any fakes? Describe them.
2. What causes people to fake it? What causes us to fake it with God?
3. Why is honesty essential—rock bottom—to our relationship with God?
4. What area of life do you find easiest to hide from God?
5. Why was David called a man after God's own heart?
6. What does "no bologna" have to do with following Jesus?

Act

Reading through the Psalms and Proverbs helps us to open up our ears to Jesus. It is helpful to read through five Psalms and one Proverb every day, allowing us to read through both books in one month.

Read

Two tremendous books for everyone who takes Jesus' call on his life seriously—especially if you intend on following Him as a disciple: Robert E. Coleman, *The Master Plan of Evangelism* (Old Tappan, N.J.: Fleming H. Revell, 1963), a classic, showing how Jesus dealt with His own disciples; Keith Phillips, *The Making of a Disciple* (Old Tappan, N.J.: Fleming H. Revell, 1981) which is the *best* I have seen on the subject of personal discipleship—a book for which I had been praying.

Appendixes

Appendix A

How to Be Discipled

> And what you have heard from me before
> many witnesses entrust to faithful men
> who will be able to teach others also.
> 2 Timothy 2:2

If reading this book has placed within your heart the desire to mature into a stable Christian man or woman, there is no better method than the one Jesus used—personal discipleship. It was also the method Paul used with Timothy. Here's how:

1. Search the Scriptures to discover what characterizes a mature Christian (Matthew 5:1–12; 1 Corinthians 13:4–7; Galatians 5:22, 23; 1 Timothy 3:1–13; Titus 1:5–9; 2 Peter 1:5–7). Make a list of these qualities, on a piece of paper.
2. Prayerfully choose someone you respect on the basis of these qualifications and ask him to meet with you weekly for prayer and Bible study. (Preferably someone within your local church.)
3. Ask him to freely point out areas of inconsistency in your life— areas of sin, neglect, rough edges.
4. Call on him for prayer or counsel, especially when you are facing temptation, spiritual warfare, or important decisions.
5. Imitate his godly habits and disciplines.
6. Be careful not to imitate his own, unique personality traits and style of ministry. Understand that you are never intended to be a ditto copy of anyone. Ultimately always keep your eyes on Jesus.
7. Be sure to establish a date to begin and a date to end (three months to a year is most helpful). A friendship will always outlast the period of formal discipleship, but it is better, when you begin, to plan to meet for a shorter period than to poop out.

Appendix B

How to Make a Disciple

> In these days he went out to the mountain
> to pray; and all night he continued in
> prayer to God. And when it was day, he
> called his disciples, and chose from them
> twelve, whom he named apostles.
> Luke 6:12, 13

As Christians it is always healthy to have someone *over* us to whom we are responsible and at the same time have someone *under* us whom we are discipling. Such accountability causes us to take Christ seriously.

1. We need to have a vision of the potential for spiritual maturity through personal discipleship.

It's the method Jesus used (Luke 11:1).
It's the method He told us to use (Matthew 28:18–20).
(Read through Mark's gospel, listing the principles of discipleship Jesus used with His disciples, on a sheet of paper.)

2. Prayerfully choose one person (of the same sex) to disciple, using the two qualifications used in 2 Timothy 2:2:

Faithfulness (reliability, consistency, dependability).
Ability to teach others. (Can you picture that person passing on the same material with someone else? If not, keep looking.)

3. Be sure the other person commits himself to the following minimal requirements:

To make every meeting, once every week, unless absolutely impossible.

To read all the assignments (mostly Bible reading).

To repent of all known sin, correcting his life-style wherever necessary.

4. Set definite time frame before you begin:

Beginning and ending point (three to twelve months).

Exact starting time and day for each weekly meeting (insist on starting promptly).

5. Keep your meeting centered in prayer and Bible study.

PRAYER

Share your weakness and needs.

Pray with each other as you begin or end each meeting.

Pray for each other's needs through the week.

Invite him to a group prayer meeting.

Help develop his prayer system.

BIBLE STUDY

Read through a book of the Bible each week (or every other week).

Use the questions from Appendix C.

While you're studying the Word together, be sensitive to spiritual needs in his life (family, self-worth, morals, eternal security, goals or future, friendship, guilt, temporal values, bitterness).

6. Let him see your commitment to Jesus as Lord over all of life:

Do things together socially or recreationally.

Convince the person you are discipling that he is a high priority in your life.

As you share the struggles you are facing, he will watch you reach out and trust Christ for the answers.

It takes one to make one.

Your ultimate goal is for him to come to know Christ, not simply to know you.

7. Your job is not done until the person you are discipling has successfully discipled someone else.

The threefold progression of discipleship that I have found helpful is:

FEEDING HIM

Using the preassigned study-guide questions in studying at least five different books of the Bible.

Building the consistent Christian disciplines of daily prayer and Bible study.

Helping him feel free to share his faith in Christ with unbelievers.

Begin tithing as a sign that Jesus is Lord over his finances.

HELPING HIM FEED HIMSELF

Allowing him to choose five Bible books to read for which he will arrive at his own study questions (knowing he in turn will use these questions with the next person he will disciple).

I recommend purchasing *How to Study the Bible*, by Henrietta Mears and *Halley's Handbook.*

Three questions should be content oriented and three questions should be application oriented, to unfold the meaning of each book and apply it to his life.

Help him discover his spiritual gifts.

Encourage him to begin serving through a local church.

Enable him to lead others to Christ.

HELPING HIM TO FEED OTHERS

Continue to meet with him once a month (minimum) while he is meeting with the person he is discipling.

Answer any questions; give positive affirmation and support, and most of all pray for him.

Appendix C

Bible Study Guide Questions

1. THE GOSPEL OF JOHN (TWO WEEKS)

   A. Content
      Make a list of all the names or titles given to Jesus. (Include the Scripture references.)
      What evidence is given that Jesus is God?
   B. Application
      In all that Jesus was teaching His disciples, what can you apply to your own life?
      With whom (besides Jesus) do you most closely identify?
      Memorize John 15:16 (word perfect).

2. 1, 2 TIMOTHY (ONE WEEK)

   A. Content
      What do you learn about Paul's relationship with Timothy? (Give references.)
      What evidence is there that Timothy felt inadequate?
   B. Application
      List three insights you gained into the Christian life.
      Memorize 2 Timothy 2:2 (word perfect).

3. ROMANS (TWO WEEKS)

   A. Content
      What words does Paul use to describe different aspects of the gospel? (1:16; 2:13; 3:24; 4:7; 5:10; 6:22; 8:17; 8:23; 8:29).
   B. Application
      When have you felt as if you could have written Romans 7?

List each spiritual gift in Romans 12:6–8. Define each gift and think of someone you know who has the gift.

Memorize Romans 12:1, 2 (word perfect).

4. 1 JOHN (ONE WEEK)

A. Content

List ten different qualities that should characterize every Christian life (give references).

What was John's purpose in writing this book? How was it helpful to his original audience?

B. Application

How are we told to respond to sin in our lives?

Bottom line—on what are we to base the knowledge of our salvation?

Memorize 1 John 5:11–13 (word perfect).

5. GENESIS (TWO WEEKS)

A. Content

What five areas of life were affected by sin in chapters three and four?

Find and list the references to the ten times you read "The generations of . . ." or "The descendents of. . . ."

Genesis is a book of origins and beginnings. See how many beginnings you can list.

B. Application

For which character in Genesis do you have the most respect?

What attribute of God is seen most clearly in Joseph's life?

Memorize Genesis 1:1; 2:24 (word perfect).

6. EXODUS

A. Content

Compare and contrast Moses' relationship with God and Pharaoh's relationship with God.

What qualities do you see in Moses? What qualities do you see in the people of Israel?

B. Application

What similarity do we see between Passover and Christ's death on the cross? (1 Corinthians 5:7).

List the Ten Commandments and make application with each of them to our contemporary society and your personal life.

Memorize the Ten Commandments.

7. LUKE

A. Content

What principle of discipleship did Jesus use with His disciples? Describe the Pharisees. Why did Jesus have such problems with them?

B. Application

List all the references to prayer. In what circumstances did they pray? What results did they see to their prayers?

List all references to women in the book.

Which words of Jesus' seemed most impressive to you?

Which deeds of Jesus' most clearly showed His love for people?

Memorize Luke 11:9–13 (word perfect).

8. ACTS

A. Content

Outline the book geographically, using Acts 1:8 as the key.

What event seems most miraculous to you?

B. Application

With which character can you most closely identify? Why?

List each place you find people praying.

Compare the early church with the church you attend.

List at least five distinctions.

Memorize Acts 4:11 (word perfect).

9. REVELATION

A. Content

In chapters two and three list the churches, identifying their good and bad qualities.

List all the *sevens* in the book.

After reading the book, describe the way Jesus appears and functions today.

B. Application

List verses under each of these major themes:

Jesus is Lord.

Satan is defeated.

The church is triumphant.

Memorize Revelation 12:11 (word perfect).

10. HEBREWS

A. Content

What is the dominant theme in the book? Describe the needs of the Christians to whom the book was written.

List the Old Testament Jewish words that are used to illustrate what Christ has now done for us.

B. Application

What situations has God used to discipline you?

Define *faith.* In what areas of your life do you still find unbelief?

Memorize Hebrew 12:1, 2 (word perfect).

11. GALATIANS

A. Content

What problems did these Christians have, from listening to false teachers?

What is to be included in "the gospel"? What is not to be included?

B. Application

Define in your own words *flesh, Spirit.*

Which "works of the flesh" are still active in your life?

List the elements of the fruit of the Spirit. Grade yourself from one to ten (one – nonexistent; ten – full bloom).

Memorize Galatians 6:7–9 (word perfect).

12. JONAH

    A. Content
       Title each chapter.
       What does God want from Jonah?
       What does God want from the people of Nineveh?
    B. Application
       How did God's feelings for Nineveh differ from Jonah's? How
       should we feel toward those outside Christ?
       What attribute of God do you see in each chapter?
       Memorize Jonah 2:7 (word perfect).

13. 1 CORINTHIANS

    A. Content
       List five church problems in Corinth, with references.
    B. Application
       Memorize chapter thirteen (word perfect).

14. 1, 2 PETER

    A. Content
       To whom is Peter writing?
       What themes does Peter deal with? How would these be particu-
       larly helpful to his audience?
       What difference do you see between 1 and 2 Peter?
    B. Application
       What sort of trials have you faced? What verse or truth in Peter
       brings strength and reassurance?
       Define *grace* as used by Peter.
       Memorize 1 Peter 5:6–9 (word perfect).

15. JOSHUA

    A. Content
       What qualities of leadership do you find in Joshua?
       What was Joshua's greatest obstacle? What was his greatest asset?

B. Application
List the references everywhere you find "the Lord said to Joshua."
What does this tell us about Joshua's life?
What sins do we find described in the book?
Memorize Joshua 1:8, 9 (word perfect).

You might find it helpful to use these questions in a small group—doing the reading and digging as homework and coming together to share and review.

Appendix D

How to Break the Boldness Barrier

I believe in street evangelism—telling people cold turkey what Jesus means to me. If you break the boldness barrier this way, telling friends and family is a lot easier. Here are seven steps I have taught in every church where I have ministered.

1. WE MUST KNOW THE SCRIPTURES.

A. Man is sinful (Romans 3:23; 6:23; Galatians 6:7; Isaiah 53:4–6).
B. Jesus is the *only* way (John 14:6; Acts 4:12; 1 Timothy 2:5).
C. You must receive (John 1:12; Revelation 3:20; Romans 10:9, 10).

2. PRAY.

Confess any known sins.
Be filled with the Holy Spirit.
Ask for God to lead you to the right person with whom to share the gospel.

3. GO TO TALK ABOUT JESUS.

A. *Going:* A thousand-mile journey starts with one step. Referring to evangelists, Paul said, ". . . How beautiful are the feet of those who preach the good news!" (Romans 10:15). The Great Commission deliberately starts with the word *go*.

B. *To Talk:* We must purpose in our hearts that our mission is to represent Jesus Christ as His ambassadors (2 Corinthians 5:17–21). We need to verbalize Christ; a silent witness is not enough.

C. *Jesus:* To talk about church, morals, or politics doesn't count. Jesus said, "And I, when I am lifted up from the earth, will draw all men to myself" (John 12:32). We need to make Jesus the issue, not a pet doctrine or point of controversy.

4. SEEK A RESPONSE.

Rather than trying to cram things down his throat, we need to be sensitive to his needs and to his mind. Asking perceptive questions is the best way to start.

"What do you think about Jesus? Is He a good teacher, a lunatic, or the Son of God?"

"If you died tonight and went to stand before God, and He asked you why He should let you into heaven, what would you tell Him?"

"Have you ever asked Jesus into your life?"

"What is the most important thing in your life? Does it really satisfy your needs?"

5. TELL WHAT GOD SAYS ABOUT JESUS IN THE BIBLE.

A. Describe His earthly life and the miracles He performed, which helped people.

B. He claimed to be the Son of God.

C. He was killed for our sins.

D. He rose from the dead and is alive right now.

E. *The Four-Spiritual Laws* (published by Campus Crusade) is very helpful.

6. TELL ABOUT YOUR OWN PERSONAL EXPERIENCE.

A. Before conversion: personally identify with the needs of unbelievers.

B. Conversion: explain exactly how you received Christ.

C. Since conversion: give at least three benefits of knowing Jesus.

7. Bring Him to a Decision.

"What are you going to do with Jesus?"
"Would you like to ask Jesus into your life?"
"Could we pray together right now?"

It is not your job to convert anyone or even convince him that he is sinful. All we need to do is tell the truth and leave the results with God.

Appendix E

Nine Icebreakers

1. I have known you for a long time, yet I have never told you about the most important thing in my life. Would you mind if I shared this with you right now?
2. Do you ever pray? When? [Usually when things go bad.] Do you feel as if your prayers are getting through? (past the ceiling?) You know, that's the way it always was for me until I met Jesus personally and now....
3. Do you ever go to church? Do you like it? Get anything out of it? [Usually not.] You know, that's the way it always was for me, until I met Jesus personally and now....
4. Do you believe in God? What do you think of Jesus Christ? Was He a good teacher, a lunatic, or the Son of God? Would you mind if I showed you what it says in the Bible about who Jesus is?
5. Do you know without any doubt that if you died tonight, you would go to heaven? If you died tonight and went and stood before God, and He said, "Why should I let you into heaven?" What would you say? Are you afraid to die?
6. What is the most important thing in your life? Does it satisfy you?
7. We've all had friends who have let us down. But, you know, I have one friend who never lets me down....
8. This has been a rough time for you, hasn't it? May I show you something Jesus said that has been real helpful to me?

9. Have you ever heard of the *Four Spiritual Laws?* They are four helpful things for us to understand about our relationship with God.
   Would you mind if we looked at them together?

Appendix F

Seven Steps in Follow-up

When you lead someone to Jesus, you are responsible to that person
just as a mother is to a newly born baby. How cruel it would be for a
mother to leave a baby without food or care! It is equally cruel for a spiritual parent to leave a "newborn babe" without spiritual food and care.
Just as babies are hungry for milk, so new Christians long to be taught
about this new spiritual life they have begun.

1. EXPLAIN WHAT HAS JUST HAPPENED, WITH JOY.

"Oh, John, I am so happy for you. Just this minute you became a child
of God. . . ." Explain:

   A. Justification (Romans 3:23; 5:6, 8, 10): "Your sins are totally for-
      given."
   B. Regeneration (1 John 5:11, 12): "You have received the life of Jesus;
      you've been born again."
   C. Reconciliation (2 Corinthians 5:18): "You are made one with God."
   D. Redemption (Hebrews 9:12): "You have been set free from sin so
      that you can now obey the living and true God."

2. EXPLAIN THAT GOD DISCIPLINES HIS CHILDREN (HEBREWS 12:3–11).

"Jesus told a story about a man who sowed seed in different types of
soil. The seed represented the gospel, and the soil represented different
types of lives. The story shows how some people who receive the gospel
lose interest because trials scorch out the Word [Mark 4:5, 6, 16, 17].

Now that you are God's child, He is going to treat you as a child by disciplining you. You must be sure to respond to trials properly."

    A. Submit to them rather than rejecting them (James 1:2).
    B. Thank God for them (1 Thessalonians 5:17, 18).
    C. Realize that they have a purpose in your life, even if you can't see it (Romans 8:28).

3. Encourage Him to Tell Others of His Conversion.

See Matthew 10:32: "If you acknowledge me before men, I will acknowledge you before my Father." Romans 10:9: "If you confess with your lips that Jesus is Lord, and believe in your heart. . . ." It is important that he tells other family and friends. Words confirm the fact of conversion in his own life.

4. Introduce Him to Other Christians.

This immediately makes him a part of his new family. "Hey, Frank, this is John. He just asked Jesus into his life." In Acts 9:17 Ananias did this with a well-known new convert, "Brother, Saul. . . ." Go on to stress the importance of fellowship with other Christians (Hebrews 10:25; Ephesians 4).

5. Encourage Him to Have a Daily Time of Reading the Bible and Praying.

Bible
    A. Make sure he has a Bible (if not get him one).
    B. Suggest a starting point: "Why don't you start in John?"
    C. Suggest *how to* read it "Ask the question 'who is Jesus?' and write down your findings."
    D. Pick a time to get back together to review the findings.

Prayer
    A. It's just like talking to another person.
    B. Being a Christian is a love relationship with Jesus Christ, so express your love to Him.

C. Find out some area in his life you can pray about for him.

D. Give him something he can pray for you about.

6. BAPTISM BY WATER SHOULD BE ENCOURAGED.

Jesus clearly taught that a part of discipleship is water baptism after conversion (Matthew 28:19). We are taught to ". . . Repent, and be baptized . . ." (Acts 2:38).

Baptism is the outward expression of what has taken place inwardly; going under the water is representative of joining Christ in His death, and the coming out of the water shows the life of Jesus in us. It is meant to be a public expression of turning away from the old life into the new.

7. MAKE ARRANGEMENTS TO SEE HIM SOON.

Make sure that you have his full name, address, and phone number. "If it's okay, I'll give you a call this week." Follow-up is essential.

A brief, helpful booklet is *Lessons on Assurance* (put out by NavPress), written in workbook form. We use it with all new Christians. As it contains five practical lessons, such a five-week study would be useful in grounding the new convert.